*Morality and Purpose*

## STUDIES IN ETHICS AND THE
## PHILOSOPHY OF RELIGION

The Series is meant to provide an opportunity for philosophical discussions of a limited length which pursue in some detail specific topics in ethics or the philosophy of religion, or topics which belong to both fields. For the most part, the Series will present work by contemporary philosophers. The contributors, while not representing any single philosophical school, will be in sympathy with recent developments in philosophy. Occasionally, however, unpublished material by earlier philosophers, or works of importance which are now out of print, or not easily accessible, will appear in the Series.

D. Z. PHILLIPS

# Morality and Purpose

by

J. L. STOCKS

Edited with an Introduction

by

D. Z. PHILLIPS

SCHOCKEN BOOKS · NEW YORK

*Published in U.S.A.* 1969
*by Schocken Books Inc.*
*67 Park Avenue, New York, N.Y.* 10016

*Copyright* © *J. L. Stocks* 1969

*Library of Congress Catalog Card No.* 69-17836

*Printed in Great Britain*

# Contents

BIOGRAPHICAL NOTE                                   *page* vii

INTRODUCTION                                          1

1. THE LIMITS OF PURPOSE                             15

2. DESIRE AND AFFECTION                              33

3. MORAL VALUES                                      51

4. IS THERE A MORAL END?                             70

5. THE GOLDEN MEAN                                   82

6. THE NEED FOR A SOCIAL PHILOSOPHY                  99

7. CAN PHILOSOPHY DETERMINE WHAT IS
   ETHICALLY OR SOCIALLY VALUABLE?                  117

INDEX                                               129

v

# *Acknowledgements*

I should like to take this opportunity of thanking Lady Stocks for the help and encouragement she has given me in preparing this volume.

I am grateful to the following for permission to reprint the papers in this collection: to the Editor of *The Hibbert Journal* and George Allen and Unwin Ltd for permission to reprint 'The Limits of Purpose' (October 1927), and 'Desire and Affection' (April 1929); to the Editor of *Philosophy* for permission to reprint 'Moral Values' (July 1929); to the Editor of *Proceedings of The Aristotelian Society* for permission to reprint 'Is There a Moral End?' (Supp. Vol. VIII); and to the Open Court Publishing Company for permission to reprint 'The Golden Mean' (*The Monist*, April 1931).

The above papers all appeared in *The Limits of Purpose* by J. L. Stocks, now out of print. I am grateful to Ernest Benn Ltd for permission to reprint the papers.

For permission to reprint 'On the Need for a Social Philosophy' (Vol. XXXVI, 1936) and 'Can Philosophy Determine What is Ethically or Socially Valuable?' (Supp. Vol. XV), I am grateful first to the Editor of *Proceedings of The Aristotelian Society*, and second to the Delegates of the Clarendon Press, Oxford, who published both papers in *Reason and Intuition* by J. L. Stocks, and finally, to Professor Dorothy Emmet who edited the collection, which now is also out of print. I should also like to thank Mr D. M. Evans who helped me with the proof reading.

Swansea, 1968                                                    D.Z.P.

# *A Biographical Note*

John Leofric Stocks was born in 1882. He was one of a family of eleven children and his father was vicar of a busy Midland parish, Market Harborough, at the time of his birth, later and for many years, Leicester. All the children were intelligent. With the help of scholarships and the benefactions that clerical families could command, all the boys went to public schools, all but one to Oxford. Family finances were strained, and when the boys became salary-earners they helped to finance the higher education of the girls. Both at Rugby, and later at Oxford, J. L. Stocks forged personal links which brought him into touch with the early movement for adult education, as well as social service, and left-wing politics. His closest contemporary friends were William Temple and R. H. Tawney. Throughout his later life he always found time for active participation in all these causes.

After graduating from Corpus Christi College he became a fellow of St. John's; and it was from there, in 1913, that he married Mary Brinton, a student of the London School of Economics, who shared his out-of-college interests and participated in all of them. His support of the women's suffrage movement and his initiative in securing the admission of women to Oxford University membership was an added bond of sympathy. His career at Oxford was, however, broken by four years of war service as an infantry officer in the course of which, having survived the Somme campaign, he was severely wounded soon after in a skirmish which won him a D.S.O. and secured for him a home-service officer-training job until demobilization in January 1919.

In 1924 he succeeded Samuel Alexander as Professor of Philosophy in Manchester. Here he found wide scope for his very varied interests. Apart from his adult-education and social-service activities, he was a keen student of international affairs and made, as soon as post-war conditions made travel to Germany possible, a close study of post-war Germany and its problems. At home, he enjoyed the company of his three children then in the early stages of education. He was also a keen theatre-goer, and in connection with the Manchester University Settlement, an amateur actor. The years 1924–1936 spent in Manchester, were probably the happiest of his life. Its response to the personality of a philosopher-citizen was warm-hearted; its social problems were challenging; its liberal intellectual climate as typified by the *Manchester Guardian* under C. P. Scott's régime, was wholly congenial.

In 1936 he was appointed to the Vice-Chancellorship of Liverpool University. University administration had always been one of his interests and the new office promised it full scope. His reign opened brilliantly. It was abruptly closed in June 1937 by his sudden death while on an adult-education tour in South Wales. His war wound had left an unsuspected internal scar for which his heart, overworked during twenty years of strenuous life, paid the penalty.

J. L. Stocks, in addition to possessing a powerful intellect and a loveable personality, possessed also remarkable physical grace and beauty.

M.D.S.

# Introduction

I was fortunate enough to be introduced to J. L. Stocks's writings on moral philosophy when I was an undergraduate. Ever since I have been puzzled by the lack of attention given to his work by contemporary moral philosophers. When I found that Stocks's papers were no longer easily accessible, I was happy to have the opportunity and the privilege of bringing seven of them together for the first time in one volume. The papers I have chosen have a thematic unity, one which is expressed in the title. In introducing them, I have been concerned in the main to bring out what I take to be the most important features of Stocks's contribution to moral philosophy. To a lesser extent, I have tried to indicate how what he has to say is a much needed corrective to contemporary moral philosophy. In emphasizing the former rather than the latter objective, I hope to present a collection of papers on moral philosophy which will be studied, not only by contemporary students, but also, as it deserves to be, by future students.

J. L. Stocks was interested in the difference moral considerations make to human action. How do moral questions enter into our assessment of actions? Stocks could say at the time he wrote these papers, and the same could be said today, that 'From the time of Aristotle to the present day it has been more or less common form among philosophers to regard purposive action as the summit of human achievement on the practical side. Man was the rational animal, and in the field of conduct he proved his rationality so far as he made his action a well-conceived step towards a clearly-defined end' (p. 15). Stocks argued, however, that the importance of moral considerations, or of artistic and religious considerations for that matter, cannot be understood or accounted for in terms of purposive action. The distinction between means and ends is central in purposive action. The means are the 'well-conceived step towards a clearly-defined end'. In themselves the means are relatively unimportant. They are important only in so far as they lead to the proposed end. A purposive view of action, then, involves taking an abstract view of action: one element in the situation is abstracted from it, namely, the end in view, and all else is made subordinate to it. This implies that the importance of the means is not only assessed by whether in fact it does lead to the proposed end, but also by the economy and amount of effort and energy it involves. If alternative means can be found which achieve the same end with greater economy and less effort and energy, the former means are cast aside without remorse or regret (see p. 38). If someone wanted to account for moral considerations in terms of purposive action, while wanting at the same time to preserve some kind of distinctiveness for moral considerations, he might argue that morality brings to action purposes of its own, or a clearer view of the purposes in hand. This Stocks will not allow: 'The goodness of a good man does not depend on this, that he has a different end from a bad man, or a clearer view of the same end, or a single end where he has many' (p. 58). What, then, does Stocks take the distinctive contribution of morality to action to be?

Consider the following example. A man may discover a brilliant and legally admissible way of making money. The prospects are great and the profit envisaged sure. Yet morality says, 'Not that way'. Perhaps the proposed way of making money involves betraying a friend. For someone with eyes only for the end and the best means for attaining it, the moral prohibition will seem arbitrary and close to madness. But what if he asked the person involved to justify his conviction that it was wrong to betray his friend? Is it not 'difficult to get beyond the simple formula that one recoils from the thought of so acting in the given situation' (p. 28). We see that the moral contribution to the action 'At a certain point, without rhyme or reason, ... makes a man see a barrier he cannot pass; he can only say that he does not consider himself free to improve the situation in just that way' (p. 28).

The above example illustrates why it will not do to think of moral considerations as providing purposes of their own, or a clearer view of purposes already given. What they do is to give attention to details which are unimportant from the point of view of purposive action.

> The moral attitude is essentially a concern for the rightness of action. A true instinct exhibits it as interfering with the execution of purpose in stigmatising as immoral the doctrine that the end justifies the means. The phrase implies that morality requires that all means shall be justified in some other way and by some other standard than their value for this or any end: that however magnificent is the prospect opened out by the proposed course of action, and however incontestable the power of the means chosen to bring this prospect nearer, there is still always another question to be asked: not a question whether in achieving this you will not perhaps diminish your chances of achieving something still more important; but a question of another kind. 'There is a decency required', as Browning said; and this demand of decency is prepared to sacrifice, in the given case, any purpose whatever (p. 77).

Purpose was concerned only with the end in view and the most economic means of realizing it. But there are other elements in the situation which the purposive view takes no account of. While men are engaged in various activities they develop a regard, not only for specific ends and the surest ways of attaining them, but also for character in action, ideals of behaviour, ways of doing things, which cannot themselves be explained in terms of the distinction

between means and ends. If one asks why men should have
a regard for such ideals and standards of behaviour, one can
only reply that they do, that is all.

But many philosophers have not been content with this
answer. They have wanted an answer to the question, Why
should I be moral? Stocks discusses some of them, like
Green and Bradley, who, it must be remembered, were
searching for an alternative to Utilitarianism. They thought
they could overcome the main objections to thinking of
morality in terms of the distinction between means and
ends, and yet retain an account of morality which is essentially purposive. They agreed that a purposive interpretation of moral action which involves a *contingent* relation
between means and ends must be rejected. But if the end of
moral action is self-affirmation or self-realization, they suggested, a purposive interpretation of morality can be
endorsed. My present state, as exemplified in the moral
actions I now perform, is not a mere means, since it is itself
part of the greater whole which is the end of my actions,
namely, self-realization. On the other hand, in so far as this
'greater self' (conceived of in different ways by different
philosophers) has not yet been attained, a reference to
future results is still justified. The development of character
thus breaks down the externality of the means–ends relation.

The above attempt to establish an internal relation between
means and ends does not escape Stocks's criticisms. He
points out that no single end, including that of one's own
moral development, can guarantee the rightness of one's
actions, and that among the many ends men aim for, one's
own moral perfection is not the highest (see p. 78). To
those who think that Stocks's worries about these matters
are unnecessary, and that obviously the man who spurns a
legally admissible way of making money *is* seeking a higher
purpose, namely, his own moral perfection, Stocks replies:

> that the act must first be shown to be right now before it can
> be relied upon to build up righteousness in the future; and—
> more relevantly to our present enquiry—that there may well be
> such an aim, and it may well be considered more important than

riches, but that it is after all only an end, like any other, a possible result of action, and that it falls with all other ends, under the inflexible moral rule that it may not be pursued by any and every means. Morality may call on a man at any moment to surrender the most promising avenue to his own moral perfection (p. 29).

Stocks does not give as many examples to illustrate his points as he might have done, and the examples he does give sometimes lack force. Perhaps the following example will serve to bring out the force of his reply. Consider a case of two friends who want to break with their way of life as prostitutes. Only one of them has the resolution to do so. She knows that to stay means going to pieces sooner or later. But she also knows that her going means that her friend would lose the little genuine affection and worth her life possesses. Her friend begs her not to go. There is little hope that things will change, that her friend will muster enough resolution to leave one day. On the contrary, it is pretty certain that if she stays, they will both be dragged down. Yet, she decides to stay. It might be said that she rejected the most promising avenue to her own moral perfection, but many would find her decision admirable nevertheless.

Some philosophers today, while differing from Green and Bradley in other respects, also look for an alternative to Utilitarianism while wanting to retain an account of moral considerations in terms of purpose. They too want an answer to the question, Why should I be moral? They suggest that an answer to this question can be found by showing how the virtues constitute a good to the just man, or by showing how what are regarded as virtues are connected to the needs of man. What is hoped for is a positive theory of human nature.[1] Just as a plant needs certain things in order to flourish, might it not be the case that man needs certain

[1] I am thinking especially of Mrs. Philippa Foot and Miss G. E. M. Anscombe's writings on ethics. See P. R. Foot's 'Moral Beliefs', *Proceedings of The Aristotelian Society* LIX (1958–59) and G. E. M. Anscombe's 'Modern Moral Philosophy', *Philosophy* XXXIII (1958).

things in order to flourish too? The actions which would satisfy those needs would be actions which men *ought* to perform. Thus, a perfect marriage between morality and rationality is brought about. The positive theory of human nature is thought of as essentially descriptive, and to say that something ought to be done would be to state an obvious fact. The troublesome barrier between facts and values would be broken down. Indeed, advocates of this view tend to deny that there is any reason to speak of *moral* obligation or of *moral* goodness. What needs elucidation is the way in which certain kinds of actions are in men's interests and others not. These philosophers are contemporary examples of the kind of moral philosophers Stocks refers to as adherents to the principle of Aristotle's Golden Mean. In relation to conduct, Stocks sees the principle implying that:

> desires and emotions are neither good nor bad, but are material, in itself neutral, out of which, by certain different arrangements and adjustments to environment, what we call goodness and badness is made: that the positive achievement which we call goodness comes, not by elimination of certain elements as bad, or by the introduction of some new factor which is the soul of goodness, but simply by the right arrangement and adjustment of these materials (p. 87).

Why do philosophers find the doctrine of the Golden Mean so attractive? Stocks remarks that 'In ethics it seems to hold out the promise of fairly meeting two demands which I think we are most of us nowadays inclined and entitled to make of an ethical theory; that it shall exhibit virtue or goodness as a positive achievement, and not as a mere negation, and that it shall offer an escape from the dualism of the moral and the natural which unsystematic reflection on the problem of conduct is apt to fall into, not without support from ethical writers' (p. 89). Today we speak in terms of the dualism between facts and values. It is significant that those contemporary moral philosophers who advocate a revival of ethical naturalism do so, partly, because of a desire to avoid talk about 'evaluative meaning' and the 'commendatory force' of

6

moral utterances.[1] They deny that there is any need to
appeal to any realm of evaluative meaning beyond the realm
of facts. Stocks would agree with this. Where he would
disagree with them is in their assumption that the only
alternative to talking of a special kind of meaning called
evaluative meaning, is to give an account of morality in
terms of purposive action. Stocks stressed that it is wrong to
think of moral considerations as being independent of purposive action. In so far as the action has an end in view,
moral action is purposive. But the moral importance of the
action will be explained by reference to features of the
action for which the agent has a regard. These ideals in
action cannot be accounted for in terms of adjusting or
arranging men's interests into some kind of hierarchy, a
hierarchy which perhaps reflects the 'true' interests of the
agent. Stocks brings out these facts very clearly.

First, the reference to the self in moral considerations is
purely contingent. Whether there is any such reference at
all will depend on the circumstances in which moral action
and moral judgement are called for. If we insist that every
moral action must be justified in terms of the agent's interests, we shall find that self-denial and self-sacrifice have
been reduced 'by some spurious arithmetic to cases of self-
seeking' (p. 95).[2] But no such justification is satisfactory or
called for.

> Are we to think, as some moralists have thought, that it is the
> fear of the pains of self-reproach or the love of the delights of
> self-approbation that makes men moral? Every unsophisticated
> mind will be against us here, and will agree rather with Marcus
> Aurelius in preferring the man who 'has no conception that he
> has done anything whatever, but may be compared to the vine
> that bears her grapes and seeks nothing more when once she has
> done her work and ripened her fruit' (p. 68).

Nevertheless, Stocks is not suggesting that the self has no
part in moral deliberation. In so far as one is dissatisfied

[1] Such talk is prominent in R. M. Hare's writings on moral philosophy.

[2] For a discussion of such reductionism see D. Z. Phillips, 'Does it Pay To
Be Good?', *Proceedings of the Aristotelian Society*, Vol. LXV, 1964–65.

with oneself, one is being called on all the time to try to be more decent. But this call cannot be described as egoism or altruism, since it is the call of morality itself. It is connected with what Spinoza called 'the effort to persevere in one's own being' (p. 69).

Second, the reference to the ideals of human action cannot be explained in terms of organizing the chaos of human interests, since the picture it creates of the agent confronted by a range of commensurable goods is alien to many situations in which we are called upon to fulfil important moral obligations. For Stocks, all theories based on such explanations stop short at the frontiers of morality. In terms of such theories, moral deliberation and calculation come to much the same thing. The only question of ultimate importance is whether some actions affect the agent's interests more or less than others. In other words, moral considerations on this view can be explained in terms of *desire*.

> For desire what is significant is the general character which enables a given individual to provide the appropriate satisfaction, the eatability of the roll of bread, the drinkability of the glass of wine. The object of desire is the mere vehicle of a motion which ends in the organism in which it begins. This means that any individual object offered for use in the satisfaction of desire may be replaced without loss or disturbance by some other individual object possessing the same general character. Discrimination between one instance and another is at most a matter of degree: this is more eatable or drinkable than that. The impulse at once fastens, without remorse or regret, on that which is placed higher in the scale. Desire is essentially transferable or vagrant as between individuals of the appropriate kind, and its valuations are necessarily relative (p. 38).

But, clearly, desire does not account for all the important features of life.

> If this were a complete account of human nature the world would be a very different place from what it actually is. If desire and its service were the whole of life there would be no fondness for places and buildings, no contemplative enjoyment of sights and sounds, no ties of affection and friendship, but only the con-

tinual grasping calculation of something to be got from men and things as they served a more or less transient need. The convenience of a utensil would be the highest form of praise (pp. 39–40).

Desire is not the only principle at work in human nature. There is also the principle of *affection*. Affection concentrates on the individual and the particular. 'The wife or mother, good or bad, is an individual significant by her individuality' (p. 38). Desire, on the other hand, abstracts and generalizes. The notion of commensurable goods is alien to affection. Affection recognizes special obligations born of special relationships. Unless this is recognized a great many moral dilemmas will be distorted and not understood. Consider the following example which Wittgenstein discussed on one occasion. The example concerns a man who has come to the conclusion that he must either leave his wife or abandon his work in cancer research. Wittgenstein said something like this about the problem:

> Such a man's attitude will vary at different times. Suppose I am his friend, and I say to him, 'Look, you've taken this girl out of her home, and now, by God, you've got to stick to her'. This would be called taking up an ethical attitude. He may reply, 'But what of suffering humanity? how can I abandon my research?' In saying this he may be making it easy for himself: he wants to carry on that work anyway. (I may have reminded him that there are others who can carry it on if he gives up.) And he may be inclined to view the effect on his wife relatively easily: 'It probably won't be fatal for her. She'll get over it, probably marry again', and so on. On the other hand it may not be this way. It may be that he has a deep love for her. And yet he may think that if he were to give up his work he would be no husband for her. That is his life, and if he gives that up he will drag her down. Here he may say that we have all the materials of a tragedy; and we could only say : 'Well, God help you'.[1]

How perverse it would be if someone confused desire and affection in Wittgenstein's latter description of the hus-

[1] See Rush Rhees, 'Some Developments in Wittgenstein's View of Ethics', *Philosophical Review*, January 1965, pp. 22–23.

band's dilemma! If one thinks it is a matter of deciding what one wants most, one cannot begin to see what the difficulty is. Imagine someone saying, 'Get another job', or 'Get another wife who'll be prepared to accept the situation'. What has he missed? Is it not the fact that the dilemma is inexplicable apart from *this* woman and *this* vocation involved in it? The reference to the husband is incidental in what has to be decided. His love of his wife and his love of his work are the important factors.

What Stocks stresses again and again is that the moral values for which people have a regard cannot be explained satisfactorily in terms of a scale of interests or in terms of basic human needs. The values are adhered to for their own sakes, because they are what they are. People often think otherwise because in a moral dispute what is stressed are details, consequences, which each party thinks the other might have overlooked. This emphasis on consequences leads one to suppose that 'the whole dispute can be reduced to a question of means and ends' (p. 81). But these details and consequences once brought to light await evaluation in terms of values and conceptions of importance which cannot themselves be explained in terms of them. For Stocks, judgements made in terms of these values are intuitive and cannot be argued. Stocks saw that the philosophers of his day who were prepared to account for moral considerations in terms of purposive action, were influenced, not merely by Utilitarianism, but by Aristotle, who regarded action as being essentially purposive, and recognized no higher practical category than that of the good to which an action is the means. The same influences are to be seen in much contemporary moral philosophy. Stocks contrasts his own view with them, describing it as a non-utilitarian and intuitive ethic. The latter description has traditional difficulties, but I do not see that Stocks inherits them. As far as I can see, he called his ethics intuitive because he refuses to seek 'ultimate' justifications, rationalizations, or explanations in non-moral terms, of moral beliefs. It is this which contrasts his views with recent movements in ethics. Reading him, for me, was like discovering a reinstatement of morality in philosophy.

Stocks also raises the question of the relation between moral philosophy and the ways in which moral considerations enter people's lives. He says that people have no right to expect philosophers to legislate on moral matters. Stocks compares the relation of the philosopher to the moral agent with the relation of the philosopher to the scientist. Philosophy cannot legislate for science. If science trespasses in the realm of metaphysics, that is another matter, but 'in practice the fact is evident that the scientific world is self governing and will not submit to the dictation of philosophy' (p. 108). Similarly, Stocks claims, it is not the business of philosophy to exhort on moral matters. If the philosopher does exhort or advocate, his philosophy becomes impure. Often, in doing so, the philosopher falsifies the facts. There is an enormous gap between the diversity of people's moral beliefs 'and the tidy ethical systems which philosophers offer us as the result of their reflection upon it. The philosopher does not trouble much to show the steps by which from that starting-point he arrived at this result. It often seems as though he had been content to generalize from his own limited practical experience, assuming that it was typical or authoritative' (p. 124).

While one might agree with the main point Stocks is making, there is reason to doubt whether moral practice and philosophical reflection can be held apart so completely as Stocks suggests. While it may not be the purpose of ethics to influence conduct, the fact remains that many moral theories have had such an effect. Moral beliefs may be based on conceptual presuppositions, for example, on presuppositions concerning the common good. A criticism or refutation of such presuppositions may lead to a change in moral beliefs. Once it is admitted that conceptual confusion can have moral consequences, one can see how practice and reflection may be interwoven, how moral and conceptual clarification may come to much the same thing in this context.

Stocks's remarks on the positive contribution of philosophy to practical affairs are less happy. The task of social philosophy is to make explicit the fundamental principles which, according to Stocks, underlie moral action:

> The only sense in which philosophy can be said to determine what is ethically or politically valuable is this, that in its critical examination of the practice and in its exposition of its principles it is attempting to make explicit and evident assumptions as to the nature of good which are for the practitioner largely concealed within the concrete detail of his judgements and decisions (p. 128).

Stocks claims that it is important to remind man of the principles underlying human conduct. 'The man of action has little leisure or inclination to discuss the principles on which he acts. . . . When men do not know the faith by which they live, they will be apt inadvertently to betray it' (p. 115). In all this, however, philosophy is not legislative, since the principles made explicit are said to be those which are in fact implicit in conduct. They are not the creation of philosophers. If men cared little for the consistency of their principles, the philosopher's indication of whether they are deviating or not from such principles would matter little. But since men do care about the consistency of their conduct, the philosopher's exposition can have an enormous influence.

Stocks's hopes for a philosophical exposition of the fundamental moral principles are based on a falsification of the facts. They seem to depend on viewing the vast variety of ways in which moral considerations enter people's lives as manifestations of a greater whole called 'moral action'. According to Stocks:

> the would-be theorist of conduct has to face the mass of material above described and attempt to reduce it to some degree of order. He has to show that this multiplicity is at bottom a unity, that this unorganized sequence of decisions and judgements has

none the less its own inner organization and can be plausibly
regarded as the expression of a single principle or of a few fundamental ideas which are in intelligible relation to one another
(p. 125).

In this task the philosopher 'will be telling the practical
man what he really is aiming at all the time' (p. 123). As a
result Stocks thinks it will be possible to show men their
moral confusions. For example, adherents to Marxism can
be shown to be wrong, not by offering them a rival utopia,
'but by showing them on the evidence of the actual achievements of humanity what man's fundamental beliefs really are'
(p. 116). But we need to stress, as against Stocks, that the
different moral beliefs people hold are not parts of something called Morality; they are what they are. There may be
points of contact between the moral views of Genghis Khan,
St. Paul, Nietzsche, or James Joyce, in so far as one calls
them *moral* views at all, but the differences are likely to be
far greater than the similarities. Any hope of reducing their
views to an 'underlying unity' is futile, and the supposition
that anything they may have in common is therefore fundamental in their beliefs, is unfounded. The diversity and
multiplicity of people's moral beliefs, instead of leading
Stocks to look for an underlying unity in them, should have
prevented him from thinking that such a unity exists.
Stocks seems to be guilty of introducing the desire for
tidiness and the kind of impurity into moral philosophy
which he himself deplored.

What is obscure and perhaps mistaken in J. L. Stocks's
moral philosophy is far outweighed by his observations on
the role of morality in action, his criticisms of the means–
ends distinction and accounts of morality in terms of purpose, and his important distinction between ethics and
advocacy.

J. L. Stocks speaks directly and penetratingly on many of
the problems being discussed at present in ethics. Not only
does he give illuminating answers to these problems, but he

asks us to reconsider whether certain issues, which contemporary philosophers think important, are the fundamental questions of moral philosophy. In doing so, I believe, he stands as one of the most important writers on ethics since 1900.

D. Z. PHILLIPS

# 1

# *The Limits of Purpose*

## I

From the time of Aristotle to the present day it has been more or less common form among philosophers to regard purposive action as the summit of human achievement on the practical side. Man was the rational animal, and in the field of conduct he proved his rationality so far as he made his action a well-conceived step towards a clearly-defined end. Thus Aristotle starts his *Ethics* from the accepted view that every art and science, and equally every action and pursuit, is directed to a good, and forthwith accepts the description of the good as that at which they all aim. The definition of this good, which is the aim of the ethical enquiry, will be the definition of the great overruling purpose which holds all human activities together and to which, ideally and ultimately, every detail of each is subservient. In defining it Aristotle conceives himself not as improvising or inventing or imaginatively idealizing, but as engaged in the analysis of fact. For this purpose is generally operative even where it is not intelligently grasped; but the highest achievements of man depend upon its being clearly grasped and consciously executed: 'Surely the knowledge of it,' says Aristotle, 'is of great importance for life, like archers, if we *aim*, we shall be more likely to *hit*'.

On this view, fully developed and fully responsible activity is the enlightened choice of means to an end; and the complete statement of the grounds for any course of action will relate it to the one ultimate end, as the best contribution towards it which seems in the circumstances to be available. Room is left, of course, for levels of activity below the purposive, but not for levels above it. Below purpose we have the more obscure states called impulse, instinct, appetite, and so on, directed to nearer ends, and not necessarily involving consciousness even of those. In these purpose is rooted as thought is rooted in sensation. The parallel developments of thought and will which differentiate the human from the lower levels of animal life are preconditioned by processes of a type shared by the whole animal world. Even in the most perfectly developed human being the complete and continuous dominance of the one ultimate purpose is never achieved. The wisest of men will hunger and thirst and sleep; he will be overcome, if only for a moment, by emotion; economy of effort will lead him to trust for much to habit and rule of thumb, and to concentrate largely on ends which are not ultimate.

Purpose, then, has its lower limits. There may be room for doubt as to their precise definition; and the best way of conceiving the relation of higher and lower is here, as in the parallel case of sensation, still today a main centre of philosophical and psychological controversy. The conception of a single ultimate end is also doubtful. It is, in fact, not much favoured by modern thought; we no longer think of our ethics as the search for a definition of the supreme good. But this does not mean that the conception of human action as essentially purposive has been surrendered. It means that our ethics is less practical in aim, less directed to helping men in the perplexities of conduct, more critical and metaphysical in character. It means also that, as compared with the ancient Greeks, we moderns are sceptics and empiricists. We distrust the power of thought to formulate a reliable answer to such a question. We do not say, 'There is no moral ideal; there is no single purpose in which every purpose is fulfilled'. We say[1]: 'Life is a conflict, solved like all conflicts only by compromise; and compromises are

[1] Cf. A. E. Taylor, *The Problem of Conduct*, p. 278.

indefinable: the Heaven of fulfilled desire is at best only a vision'. Or we say[1]: 'The good, the moral ideal, is capable only of a formal and abstract definition; and the good man will be found in practice guiding himself by no hazardous attempt at a definition, but relying largely on the best judgment of his generation and concentrating his efforts without reserve on "some work of recognized utility" '. The clear-cut Greek conception of a *summum bonum* is not surrendered; still less is it replaced by another conception equally definite; it is overlaid with hesitations and reservations and qualifications until it is almost unrecognizable. The unification of the moral life in a single distinctive ultimate purpose seems to remain in the form of a 'mere idea' or unrealizable ideal.

Now I am going to suggest that much of this doubt and uncertainty arises from failing to keep separate questions that ought to be distinguished, and from obstinately continuing to group under a single term aspects of conduct which require to be kept apart. In taking as my subject the limits of purpose it is not the lower limits that I have in mind, but the upper. The lower limits are amply recognized, perhaps even at the present day exaggerated; an upper limit seems not to be effectively recognized at all. What I wish to argue is that as soon as purpose is precisely defined it becomes clear that it accounts for none of the highest human activities; that, on the contrary, the very existence of art, of morality, of religion, of genuine thought and knowledge, depends on the ability of man to rise above the level of purpose. In the higher animal, if man still claims that name, purpose in a sense supersedes appetite and impulse; in that same sense, I shall argue, these interests and activities involve the supersession of purpose. My thesis, in short, is that limits are set to purpose by art and poetry and history, by science and philosophy, by morality and by religion.

II

Clearly I must begin by giving some definition of 'purpose'.

[1] Cf. T. H. Green, *Prolegomena*, Book III, Chapter I.

By purpose I mean primarily the concentration of effort on bringing about a certain result. Its varieties are those of the results contemplated, which are called the end. If the result is sufficiently distant, e.g., if a politician of the present day is credited with the purpose of establishing a United States of Europe, the end, though particular, may be regarded as the central unifying principle of a whole life or the greater part of it. But clearly it will not account for everything in that life, even during the period of its dominance. And, besides that, there is no finality in events. The ripples of circumstance pass quickly out of sight and beyond calculation . . . Obviously a particular event, whether near or distant, can possess no absolute value.

But it is not necessary, of course, to rest in the particular. Purpose can also be conceived more generally by generalizing the result at which it aims. And so we get a notion like the greatest happiness of the greatest number. This famous phrase does not represent an ultimate infinitely distant event, but rather a *type* of result which a man may be conceived as always concentrated on in every action. Our definition of purpose is to be interpreted as including the general direction of effort to a general end or type of result such as this.

The case becomes more complicated when we turn to the formulae of self-realization. When Green tells us[1] that 'the perfection of human character—a perfection of individuals which is also that of society, and of society which is also that of individuals—is for man the only object of absolute or intrinsic value', and that this perfection consists 'in a fulfilment of man's capabilities according to the divine idea', he seems to think partly at least of a type of result to be achieved by action. When he opposes to the utilitarian formula his own doctrine as 'the theory of the good as human perfection', he clearly thinks of his good as something to be gradually realized and brought about, as an end or possible result of action. Similarly, when he is arguing for virtue rather than pleasure as the common good, he lays great

[1] *Prolegomena*, p. 293.

stress on the notion of development.[1] 'The idea of the good
is an idea of something which man should become for the
sake of becoming it, or in order to fulfil his capabilities, and
in so doing to satisfy himself.' In the complex involutions
of Green's thought there are other elements, due to the
influence of Kant, and even of Aristotle himself; but the
main stream represents the moral will as purposive in the
sense of my definition. The decisive evidence is the emphasis on development. For purpose is a forward-looking
attitude, one which scrutinizes the present for its possibilities and values it for what it can make of it.

A purposive interpretation of human action, then, will
be an interpretation of it in terms of the result or type of
result to which it is directed. If such analysis is taken as
ultimate and final, morality must be so interpreted; that is
to say, the moral factor in conduct must be explained as
devotion to a distinctively moral good or end or result. We
have already seen that explanations of morality on these
lines are actually offered, not merely by hedonists and
utilitarians, whose devotion to purpose is notorious, but
also by the Kantian and idealist philosopher, T. H. Green.
When I, on the other hand, stated as part of my thesis the
contention that the moral interest involves the suppression
of purpose, I mean to imply that this explanation is
illegitimate; that morality is not, as such, a desire to bring
anything in particular into the world, that it has no distinctive ideal, that it is not a search among the possibilities of
the present for the materials of a better world, that it
involves no notion of improvement and no ideas on evolution.

There are two features of the purposive attitude as
defined which I wish specially to emphasize because they
exhibit from different angles its essential incompleteness,
and thus indicate in advance the nature of the supplement
which it requires and the kind of transformation of which it
is capable. These are (1) that the effort and energy spent on
fulfilling a purpose are not self-justifying, but only, as it
were, excused by the result produced; (2) that there is a

[1] *Prolegomena*, pp. 283, 284.

faulty abstraction in the purposive view of a situation and of the changes made or proposed to be made in it.

Let me explain these two points rather more fully.

(1) So far as you are wholly concentrated on bringing about a certain result, clearly the quicker and easier it is brought about the better. Your resolve to secure a sufficiency of food for yourself and your family will induce you to spend weary days in tilling the ground and tending live-stock; but if Nature provided food and meat in abundance ready for the table, you would thank Nature for sparing you much labour and consider yourself so much the better off. An executed purpose, in short, is a transaction in which the time and energy spent on the execution are balanced against the resulting assets, and the ideal case is one in which the former approximate to zero and the latter to infinity. Purpose, then, justifies the efforts it exacts, only conditionally, by their fruits.

(2) My other main criticism of the purposive attitude is its highly abstract view of a situation. This follows, again, directly from the fact that purpose is a dominant interest in a result or type of result. Clearly, any feature of any situation has infinite ramifications and is capable of entering into an infinity of practical combinations; and clearly any change in a situation will have consequences inexhaustible in range and variety. Purpose assesses the situation and deals with it from a definite angle. The value of each feature is its actual or possible contribution to a single result, and this also is the sole test of the acceptability of any change proposed. Thus what is taken into account is viewed partially and abstractly, and much is forced out of sight altogether by the limitation of the point of view. This may be stated otherwise by saying that the thinking characteristic of the attitude of purpose is at the level of the class concept and the abstract universal. To such thinking the individual always presents itself as an inexhaustible complex, and unknown or unknowable. By abstraction it simplifies the problem, but at the cost of a divorce between knowledge and reality: 'The individual may exist', it says, 'but it is the universal

that is known'. In a word, for such thinking, and for purpose which is its practical embodiment, there is no individual.[1]

III

I propose now to test this challenge to purpose in the two fields of art and morality. I want to show how these two interests supplement and transform, without abolishing, the purposive attitude. I must point out by way of preliminary the limitations of the question I am asking. My question is not metaphysical. It would not be to the point to enquire as to the status in reality of the things or valuations which art and morality reveal and make manifest. The question is, rather, logical or psychological, as to the nature of the act which has a positively artistic or moral character; and, further, if, as I suppose, other factors not specifically moral or artistic enter into these acts, as to the distinctive contribution of the supervening artistic or moral interest.

I take Art first. What I have to show is that the artistic attitude supervenes upon purpose in such a way that the two cardinal defects with which I have charged purpose are in some degree abolished and made good. I must begin by showing how art enters into and modifies purpose, or, to put the same thing otherwise, in what sense I take the concrete act in which the artistic interest expresses itself to remain nevertheless purposive in character. I mean this to imply that there is no definitely and specifically artistic act or occupation, that all practice of art is simultaneously the practice of something which is not art; and to those two assertions I would further venture that, so far as I can see, there is no practice or occupation which will not accept in some degree an infusion of art. Art, in short, is an embroidery upon the fabric of human purpose; and though the fabric is sometimes more and sometimes less suitable, it is never quite hopelessly unsuitable.

[1] It is worth noticing that the thought embodied in action based on appetite is even more narrowly abstract, owing to the fixity and limitations of our appetites, e.g. hunger constitutes an interest in a situation as food-providing and in things only as foods. Cf. also fear-danger.

Let me give some illustrations. When I ride a bicycle, I have normally a purpose in riding. I want to get somewhere more quickly than I could on foot, or I want exercise for my muscles and air for my lungs. And either of these may be items in a purpose of larger scope—to 'keep fit', to improve my health, and so on. But I may also feel an affection for the machine I ride and a delight in the expertness with which I manage it. Such feelings do not in any way conflict with or prejudice any purpose I may have in riding. On the contrary, they normally assist it. What here enters is not a new purpose or a further purpose; it is the conscious enjoyment of the means and methods by which the work is done; and it is this that I regard as the distinctively artistic contribution. Common language recognizes that even the most mean and sordid occupations admit of such a development. It speaks of artists even in cruelty and in crime. A case of blackmail or murder may be a despicable act and unpleasant to contemplate, but its squalor is felt to be appreciably lessened if in it we can see an artist at work, *i.e.* if we can see the crime as the work of an expert who rejoiced in his own expertness. A similar idea underlies Burke's romantic picture of the high society destroyed by the French Revolution. He calls it an 'age of chivalry' with an 'unbought grace of life', and defends its patent weaknesses by proclaiming the 'sensibility of principle . . . which ennobled whatever it touched, and under which vice itself lost half its evil by losing all its grossness'.

The practices and occupations just mentioned are not such as are commonly associated with the term 'art'. They are cited just for that reason, to show how even there art may be said to supervene upon and transform purpose. No less plain is the substratum of purpose in the practices conventionally accepted as artistic. Speech and writing are the tools of the most popular of all the arts. They serve the purpose of communication, which is itself an ingredient in nearly every human enterprise. The artist takes this medium and exploits its resources. He is in love with his medium and delights in his mastery of it. But it would not be *language* he used if he divorced it from its proper use and purpose. He is still telling something, conveying information, and his art is only fully justified if he tells what he has to tell the better for his art. This is true even of the most rarefied verbal art, lyric poetry; but often the refinements forced on the artist by his delight in the words, and in the rhythms and patterns which they make, seem in the end to have reduced the underlying purpose to the mere shadow of a shade.

I need only remark further under this head that, in spite of the common delusion to the contrary, there is nothing specifically artistic in the representation of a visible object in another medium, e.g. in oil paint laid on canvas or a carved block of marble. The fact that such representations can be made by machinery is alone sufficient to prove this. And even when made by man these representations may be a product of a purely purposive attitude. Nearly every tradesman's catalogue gives some examples of representation untouched by art. And Scotland Yard is not made a school of art by its collection of criminals' finger-prints. No. First there was the demand for representations and a trade which arose to meet it. Then this trade transformed itself into art, and continues today to transform itself into art, to the extent to which in any given instance of its use the craftsman's delight in the medium mastered and penetrated the product.

We may say, then, generally, that in purpose art finds its opportunity, or that art is essentially parasitic upon purpose. It exists by adopting a purpose foreign to itself and exploiting the medium by which that purpose is achieved. What I have now to show is that in developing its opportunity it tends to make good the two defects of purpose already explained, or that, unlike the botanical parasite to which I have compared it, so far from stifling and eventually perhaps killing its host, it really brings it the complement which it needs.

I hardly need do more than mention what these two defects were to secure assent to the proposition that the artistic attitude does much to remove them. I complained of purpose, first, that it conferred no positive value on the effort demanded for its fulfilment, and, secondly, that it involved a highly abstract view of a situation. It is surely beyond dispute that the first limitation is corrected in the artistic attitude. The man we call an artist may be, in fact, a lazy fellow, who would like to stop working and live on the money he has saved; but the artist in him cares nothing for the money, little even for the pictures he has made, and demands only further opportunities for the exercise of his artistic gifts. The effort must no doubt be fruitful, it must be successful in producing something worth having; but, that condition satisfied or on the way to satisfaction, the effort is self-justifying.

The other point, the undoing of the abstraction enforced by the purposive attitude, needs more careful statement, because it is the root of the matter. Purpose involves, by general agreement, a distinction between the means and the end. The means represent the best available path in the circumstances to the result which is proposed as end. This involves the consequence that the process as a whole—the achieving of this result by these steps—always fails to exhibit a complete and satisfying unity. In every calculation of means there is always, and owing to the limitations of human knowledge, there must always be, wide scope left for possible alternatives. There may be a number of different tools or methods or materials which will serve the purpose, so far as we can see, equally well. For the purpose is definite and limited, and the tools, methods, and materials proposed to be used are only partially relevant to it. For instance, your purpose may involve the provision of a support for a given weight. The structure erected will necessarily possess a certain shape and colour, and the different materials suggested will no doubt differ in their possibilities of shape and colour; but these differences will be irrelevant to your purpose, so far as it involves only the provision of an efficient support. Thus, the indifferent, the equally good or serviceable, is not eliminated, with the inevitable result that the process regarded as a whole lacks real unity and cohesion.

The same defect is seen perhaps even more clearly if we consider the practical or purposive use of language for conveying necessary information. There are many ways of saying anything which 'from a practical point of view', as we say, are equally effective; as purposive beings, we perceive our vocabulary to be full of synonyms. The practical man does not stop to pick and choose his words; he finds words which will do. (Of course there is no purely practical man; every man is something of an artist, but in any pressing emergency, in which something has to be said at once, we are all flung back to the purely purposive level.) But this collection of words which will 'do' has nothing to recommend it except the purpose for which it will 'do'. It remains in loose and accidental relation to the purpose which it serves, as a mere means to it. Now the artist destroys the mere means, abolishes the indifferent or equally good, and in so doing makes of the whole complex of means and end for the first time a real organic unity. Art endows the despised means, the tools of purpose, with a significance of their own. It necessarily refuses to recognize any irrelevancy whatever; it insists that everything that enters into the process at any stage must justify itself completely on every side of its being. Every scrap of material used must be completely used up. This is, of course, an ideal which is not actually anywhere fully achieved, because nothing is perfect and art cannot fully satisfy its own demands; but one can see the tendency powerfully at work as art enters into and dominates the purposes of men. Thus for the artist in words there are no synonyms. The poet asks his reader to concede, not just that this word or phrase will do, but that it alone will do. The words have ceased to be the mere slaves of purpose. They remain its servants, but make good their right, as words, to consideration.

So far as art masters the purpose on which it supervenes, it makes each smallest detail of the execution significant; it provides a reason of its own for every choice left open by the purpose or theme. The reason, of course, cannot be

25

expounded in argument. It is impossible to prove that a word or phrase is artistically necessary. It will, however, be recognized as appropriate and significant by any reader who makes effective contact with the mind of the author, and it will be perceived or felt as necessary in proportion as he recognizes finality and perfection in the work.

This involves, further and lastly, the consequence that the transformation effected by the artistic interest is nothing less than the achievement of individuality. What purpose aims at is and must be defined in general terms; what purpose achieves is no doubt a particular state or fact, but this is justified not in its detail and particularity, but by its general conformity to the project outlined in advance. Art has no aim of its own, and any advance sketch it may put out of a projected achievement is a sketch, not a plan, and contributes nothing whatever to the evidence by which the finished work is to be judged. The achievement is the process and its product, significant in all its detail, organically united and containing its justification within itself.

## IV

It remains for me to make good my challenge in the field of morality.

In the case of art I have tried to show (1) that the concrete artistic act is purposive in character, though not *merely* purposive; (2) that the supervening artistic interest is not purposive in character, not another and a higher purpose, but parasitic on or complementary to a purpose on which it supervenes; (3) that in certain definable ways art confers on the purposive process into which it enters a fuller being and significance. I have now to urge that all these three things can be said equally of the moral act and the moral interest. With the first two points I do not propose to detain you long, not because I wish to suggest that they are beyond controversy, but because the sense in which I understand them is, I trust, sufficiently evident from what I have already said about art. The point that needs explanation most is the third, because that demands a definition of the nature of the contribution made by morality, which has to be distinguished not only from purpose, but also from art.

Purposive action may be said generally to be directed to the improvement of a situation. An intended action is intended to make things better; not necessarily better absolutely, but relatively better, i.e. such action is justified only if the situation is the better for its having occurred. Under the term 'situation' must be included anything and everything that is or may be altered by action, including such features of the agent himself. Purposive action, then, is the attempted bettering or amendment of a situation in the sense explained. Now, when the action involves what is called a moral decision, or the solution of a moral problem, it does not cease to be this; it remains purposive and must still abide judgment by results. That corresponds to my first point concerning art. Secondly, the moral contribution is not a new and further purpose. Morality does not ask us to improve situations in ways either contrary or supplementary to those which the non-moral purposive intelligence contemplates. Morality offers no new road to Utopia, nor is there any specifically moral result at which, as moral beings, men are required to aim.

I pass to the third and most difficult point—to the question, What is the nature of the distinctive contribution made by morality to purposive action?

A formal point of some importance needs to be made at once. Morality, like art, enters into action as an additional principle of discrimination; it makes distinctions of value which without it would not be made. But we have already said that it does not override or supersede the discriminations effected by purpose. If this is right, then it follows inevitably that the field of morality, like the field of art, is the area left indeterminate by the abstractions of purpose; that morality, like art, must operate by giving significance to detail which without it is insignificant, by setting a differential value on features which to purpose were indifferent or equal in value. Here arises a difficulty as to the relation with art. Purpose proposed an end and construed all else with sole reference to it; art brought the means to life and made them justify themselves. What room is left, then, for morality? Means and end between them exhaust the act, and that which is individual is a whole. If there is room for morality we know where its operation is to be looked for; but have we left room for it?

Let us now take a simple instance of moral discrimination. Suppose one rejects a possible way of making money on moral grounds. This will not mean that one gives up the purpose of making money where one decently can; it will not mean that any error has been made in the calculation on which the expectation of profit was based; it will not mean that one has thought of another and a better way of making money. Let us suppose the purpose firm, the calculation correct, and the prospect of gain more assured and more brilliant by far than that of any discoverable alternative. I suppose it will be agreed that it may still be rejected on moral grounds. How is one to describe that rejection or state those grounds? It is difficult to get beyond the simple formula that one recoils from the thought of so acting in the given situation. This recoil or repulsion is not the opposite or contradictory of the former attraction. Nothing envisaged in the merely purposive attitude as actual or probable is now disowned. All that is admitted and remains in view. But something new plainly has been seen which accounts for the change of mind. What is it? To the merely practical or purposive man, say a partner, who has followed you through your calculations and understands the projected coup in all its bearings, your rejection will seem madness, something wholly irrational, a blind subservience perhaps to ancient superstition or old-fashioned business convention, or a lazy, good-tempered acquiescence in wholly arbitrary and artificial limitations upon enterprise. The moral contribution seems to be a mere negation. At a certain point, without rhyme or reason, it makes a man see a barrier he cannot pass; he can only say that he does not consider himself free to improve the situation in just that way.

I know that there are many who will tell me that my

difficulty is imaginary; that there is a moral aim and purpose, which is the ultimate overriding purpose of life; that this man, who rejects a safe and legally admissible means of enriching himself, rejects it because he is after something more important than that, with which in the given circumstances that conflicts. He is seeking, they will perhaps say, his own spiritual development and perfection. To which I might reply that the act must first be shown to be right now before it can be relied upon to build up righteousness in the future; and—more relevantly to our present enquiry—that there may well be such an aim, and it may well be considered more important than riches, but that it is after all only an end, like any other, a possible result of action, and that it falls, with all other ends, under the inflexible moral rule that it may not be pursued by any and every means. Morality may call on a man at any moment to surrender the most promising avenue to his own moral perfection.

I return, then, to my difficulty. This impatience of the practical man with the curtailment of his activities inflicted by the intrusion of the scruples of morality has some parallel in the field of art. The artistic conscience also is apt to make itself a nuisance to the practical man. In the name of art also he finds himself adjured to choose the more troublesome and costly method where the easier and less costly would do as well. The parallel is encouraging, because it suggests that we are right in supposing some similarity between art and morality in their relation to purpose. But the parallel seems incomplete, if only for the reason that art has quite evidently its positive triumphs—triumphs which rich men will pay large sums of money to get into their possession, while those of morality are hard to find, and certainly are not bid for by millionaires.

Yet I cannot help thinking that a solution of the problem which will eventually lay this ghost is not so very far off. We have only to ask the simple question, What is the subject of the moral judgment? To this question all human experience and all reflection upon it gives one unanimous answer—Action. Action and conduct, and the human will as manifested in these, provide the field of moral discrimination. A result is not praised or blamed. The things and methods used in effecting it are not morally good or bad. Praise and blame and the predicates importing moral value are reserved for action itself, i.e. for the human will which by given means seeks a given end. Purpose, of course, when fully developed and expressed, is action, and the embroidery of art, if incidental to purpose, is incidental to action; but 'action' none the less is a term foreign to the vocabulary equally of art and of purpose.

The utilitarian, who is the practical man turned philosopher, may actually use this word, but he would have to surrender his doctrine if he meant by it what he ought to mean. What he means by action is only a particular type of result, a result which is conditioned by conscious human activity. He cannot get away from results, for results carry the only independent value which he recognizes. Morality, however, like art, cares nothing for results. To morality it does not matter what the results may be, so long as they are practically acceptable. The future result must be transformed into the present intention before it will enter into the notion of action as judged good or bad. A comparison between the moral judgment and the judgment of practical utility verifies this immediately. In the purposive attitude the emphasis is on results. Therefore the practical man must wait and see; his method is that of trial and error; his judgments must be tentative, qualified with cautious reservations for what the future may bring; in the nature of the case, he can give no last and final word. The moral value, on the other hand, is in the action itself, and the moral discrimination is absolute and decisive. The moralist gives from moment to moment a judgment which is final and irreversible. Justice is not altered though the heavens fall.

It is after all a plain fact that any process carried out by human muscles under the direction of human intelligence is a partial expression of the nature of the agent and of the relation in which he conceives himself to stand to other persons and to the rest of the world in which he lives. In such a process purpose sees only the result and all else in terms of it as means; the energy spent will be wasted unless it brings in a proportionate return. Art glorifies the means, brings them to life, and thereby also makes the expenditure of energy self-justifying. Art thus binds the process into a real unity and individuality. But art remains preoccupied with the external; of the mind and will operating in the process it takes no account.

> Demand of lilies wherefore they are white:
> Extort her crimson secret of the rose:
> But ask not of the Muse that she disclose
> The meaning of the riddle of her might.
> Somewhat of all things sealed and recondite,
> Save the enigma of herself, she knows.[1]

Morality, supervening upon purpose and art, completes the development by replacing this central fact at the centre.

Thus the progress from purpose through art to morality is at bottom a progress to a more concrete grasp of fact. The corrections and refinements induced upon purpose by these two intruders are in principle simply the corrections necessary upon a fuller and truer view of the situation. The apparent negativeness of the moral contribution is due to the fact that the human will, as moral, is engaged for the most part in merely re-affirming itself. In the concrete moral act the purposive-artistic complex is absorbed and transformed, as purpose was absorbed and transformed by art; and with this last transformation the development of the practical attitude is completed. There can be no further judgment in which this last is absorbed, for the whole fact is now present to consciousness. What came first was action, and, as such, amenable to moral judgments; but it was action that did not know itself as action, and consequently did not judge itself. But in the last stage, mediated by the intervention of art, we have action fully conscious of itself and self-justified. The moral will is the self-conscious will, satisfied and dissatisfied with itself.

[1] W. Watson, *Lachrymae Musarum*.

31

I called my subject the Limits of Purpose, and I claim that the phrase is justified, since purpose alone will not give us art or morality. I have spoken also of the supersession of purpose; and purpose *is* superseded so far as art and morality, when they enter in, take charge and have the last word. But the reader may, if he wishes, call it the completion of purpose, so long as he admits that purpose is brought to completion by something not itself.

# 2

# *Desire and Affection*

---

## I DESIRE AND THOUGHT

The simplest analysis of human action shows desire and thought co-operating in it, involved in a kind of circle, each determining the other.

Some germ of thought and knowledge must be involved in even the lowliest response to which the name 'action' is applicable. To the extent to which a creature can think and know, it can act. At its lowest, action appears to be a response to something observed. The observed may be called generally the situation; it is this that is thought about, that the creature seeks to know. We can then say, without injustice to common-sense psychology, that the range of action depends on the fullness with which the situation is grasped and understood. This means that thought and knowledge control and limit action. Thus we have one of the two relations which go to form the circle.

But it appears to be equally true that thought and knowledge are limited, though not in precisely the same way, by desire. Without desire, we suppose, that self-initiated movement which is characteristic of life would be wholly impossible. In fact, men and animals appear to be so made that they are predisposed at any moment to action on certain lines, lines laid down in general for all by nature, but specialized and modified in each individual by use and practice. Desire and instinct are the two chief heads under which these predeterminations are brought. We need not consider the relation of these two terms to one another; for common sense supposes that any predisposition that affects action affects it in the form of desire. Thus the single term desire suffices.

Now a desire, considered as operative in conduct, is essentially a selective response coupled with a selective perception. It does not matter whether what is called desire is a universal feature of animal life, like the desire to eat, or a highly specialized and developed interest, like the collector's passion for old china. Hunger not only makes a man behave in a certain way to food when he sees it; it also leads him to see it. A predisposition to act on certain lines is also a predisposition to see certain aspects of a situation more readily and prominently than the rest. The knowledge sought is sought as the condition of effective action, and the main lines of action are predetermined by desire. Desire stimulates to thinking, but also limits it.

In this way the circle is completed. Thought and desire are involved in reciprocal control and limitation. But the circle is not a closed circle. These principles, it seems, vary also independently of one another, and thus the circle is capable of enlargement.

Circumstances *force* things upon our notice, and the relevant comes to us richly contaminated with irrelevancies. From this surplus material, by slow and gradual stages the field of desire and action will be enlarged and enriched. And even if desire were completely in control of thought, in the sense that it settled always and without fail what elements in a situation should receive attention, there would still remain unsettled the question of the creature's capacity to explore the implications of the elements registered. The clues secured may be followed to any distance. Thought may to a less or greater degree interpret the present in the light of the past and as the germ of the future. The more it does so, the more extensive will be the field of action revealed, even within the limits of relevance established by desire. (There may, of course, be a compensating loss here. The diminution of the tyranny of the present, as such, may involve a diminished range and intensity of registration. But this is difficult to prove, and in any case the loss would be fully cancelled by the extension of the range of action which this enrichment of the present brings with it.) In these ways at least, if in no others, the power of thought shows in its development a certain independence of its master, desire.

At least as high a degree of independence must be claimed for desire in relation to the admitted mastery of thought. It must be remembered that when we set desire in opposition to thought as an independent principle co-operating with it, as popular psychology does, we must necessarily regard desire as unthinking or unconscious. Common language most often applies the term 'desire' to a state in which the subject of desire is conscious of what he is seeking and of the means by which it might be got. Such states are obviously conditioned by the limits of thought and knowledge. In them the conception of something as desirable is at work. But the desiring creature, considered simply as desirous, with no additional complication, is to be taken as not conscious of anything as desirable. It is desire in this simple sense that makes cattle attend to their fodder and eat it, without any consciousness, as we suppose, of what they are doing or why. Equally it is desire in this sense which makes a young man at a certain age begin to observe the feminine as such and find that factor in presented situations interesting: he need not know or think why. This last instance shows how desire may vary independently of thought and carry thought with it in its variation. By every such variation the field of action is enriched and complicated.

The circle, then, is not a closed circle. The mutually involved factors are capable to some extent of independent variation.

These two principles then, Desire and Thought, evolve together in complicated interaction on the background of human history. This is no account of mind in evolution, and the subtleties are beyond us. But let us try to seize a critical point. At some point in this long history the mind of man in its backward and forward look achieves a view of itself. It is now aware not merely of the food which it eats, but of itself as aware of the food and predisposed to grasp and eat it. It is aware for the first time of the food as food. By this step life is much complicated and altered. Thought in its first form, the form in which it was postulated as a condition of anything that deserved the name 'action', was no more practical than theoretical. It was the purposeless registration of a situation on lines prejudiced, no doubt, but unconsciously prejudiced, by the demands of the organism. The new consciousness of these demands makes a revolution and marks the beginning of practical thought. Such concepts as desire and desirable begin to appear. It is only when a living creature becomes aware of his various desires as desires and begins to notice how precarious their satisfaction is, that he finds himself face to face with a practical problem in the foreseen danger of disappointment and the pressing need of co-ordination. Reflection on this problem will naturally bring to birth by degrees such notions as interest, welfare, pleasure, happiness, under which the desires and their objects are correlated. Meanwhile, side by side with this development of practical thought, a parallel movement brings to birth by degrees out of the many unrelated desires the single sovereign will. It is a will which presupposes the desires and is directed generally to their satisfaction. The evidence for its existence is the same in principle as the evidence for the existence of a desire. The proof of the existence of a desire for food is the action of eating. Similarly, when we see a man refrain from eating when hungry, we have to postulate an overmastering desire which enables him to refrain. Another desire of the same order, say, a desire for drink, will not serve our purpose, since the attitude of the man who refuses food is one in which the desire for food is recognized and accepted as legitimate. We suppose then that there is a desire of a higher level, a desire for the truly desirable, which informs will and conditions purpose. Purpose is the characteristic expression of will as sovereign over primitive desire. The immediacy of desire, 'leaping to its prey' (to quote an eighteenth-century phrase) 'like a tiger chained by cobwebs', is replaced by a mediation, which distinguishes the means from the end and generalizes desire under the notion of good.

In mind at this stage appears for the first time that state or activity which we most commonly intend when we speak of desire as present in a person. By the word 'desire' we commonly mean a felt tension between a present situation, recognized as in some way defective, and the brighter possibilities which it suggests. Actually such an attitude, thanks to the development of thought and will, is compatible with the complete dormancy of desire in the sense in which I first used the word. A man full-fed and wholly devoid of hunger may be scheming for a better food supply and struggling with all his might to secure it. Creatures that live on more concentrated food than grass are only intermittently hungry; but their endowment of thought and will enables them to give their whole day, if they please, to the enrichment of their table. Hunger is for the animals: it is their privilege to be greedy. Greed presupposes hunger and is essentially the determination to make the most of the opportunities which hunger offers. If the word may be extended, as it often is in common speech, to cover all the senses and the desires connected with them, greed will serve as a general descriptive name for the organizing principle of life at this level. The activities of such a life will take more and less reputable forms, varying with the more and less fastidious taste of the individual: they will cover themselves in any case with respectable and even exalted names, as incidents in the pursuit of happiness or well-being, of self-realization or self-development; but in principle greed will remain an appropriate general description. For the unifying principle is nothing but the calculated effort at a systematic exploitation of the desires, with a view to getting the maximum return from them. The conception of an ultimate end, whether called by the name of happiness or by any other name, is a delusion if it is supposed that this will serve to define the maximum. Limits are set no doubt in a favourable case to the exploitation of a given desire, but only in a rough and ready fashion, by trial and error, according to the felt operation of the principle of diminishing returns.

As desire becomes rationalized and self-conscious by the governing power of thought, it reveals itself as an interest in a certain kind of object. We come to call objects which eaten will satisfy hunger, 'food', and objects which drunk will satisfy thirst, 'drink'. These names, 'food' and 'drink', are not simply general names for things which are interesting as individuals, as the name 'wife' and 'mother' apply to innumerable cases in each of which a uniquely situated individual receives the name. The wife or mother, good or bad, is an individual significant by her individuality. This is not the case with the object of desire. For desire what is significant is the general character which enables a given individual to provide the appropriate satisfaction, the eatability of the roll of bread, the drinkability of the glass of wine. The object of desire is the mere vehicle of a motion which ends in the organism in which it begins. This means that any individual object offered for use in the satisfaction of desire may be replaced without loss or disturbance by some other individual object possessing the same general character. Discrimination between one instance and another is at most a matter of degree: this is more eatable or drinkable than that. The impulse at once fastens, without remorse or regret, on that which is placed higher in the scale. Desire is essentially transferable or vagrant as between individuals of the appropriate kind, and its valuations are necessarily relative.

It follows that the type of thought which is stimulated by desire and characteristic of a life organized in the service of desire is abstract and general, attentive not to the particulars themselves, but to them in respect only of certain general characters which they may exhibit. But desire is generally supposed to be as old as human life; and it would seem to follow that the general term and the class-concept are as old as human thought. This would involve us in conflict with the view often expressed by Locke and other empirical philosophers that ideas of particular things come first and general ideas are somehow manufactured out of them. But we need not fear this conflict. There was a similar delusion in the realm of politics that the free individual came first and the ordered state came after, as a necessary and effective, but still regrettable, abridgment of his liberty. So here general ideas were a necessary and valuable economy. History and anthropology have now finally discredited this political myth, and the same solvents may be asked to do their work here. The study of history and the comparison of different levels of culture show conclusively that the grasp of the individual is not the starting-point but the goal of thought's journey.

To return then to desire. The thought of a desirous creature is on this primitive level of general terms and class-concepts, for which individuality—all that makes a person or thing the irreplaceable entity that it actually is—is either non-existent or irrelevant. In general it will be recognized that things have their differences and peculiarities; but in the operations of desire these will appear only as a surd or remainder. The attitude in its purest form is well exemplified when one of us today goes shopping among standardized manufactured articles, to buy a mowing-machine or a motor car. By previous discussion in general terms, assisted by experience of instances of the various 'makes', we can, if we are sufficiently strong-minded, decide exactly what we want; and any special peculiarities in what we get are more likely to be a ground of complaint than a source of additional satisfaction. And when we get home, if we are asked what we have done, we say we have bought *a* Ransome or *a* Morris. This is characteristic of practical thought which, concentrated on general ends, such as wealth, pleasure or happiness, remains irretrievably abstract and general in its attitude to the things and persons which it uses. So far as man is merely practical, or if practical means no more than this, the individual as such has no interest for him whatever.

If this were a complete account of human nature the world would be a very different place from what it actually is. If desire and its service were the whole of life there would be no fondness for places and buildings, no contemplative enjoyment of sights and sounds, no ties of affection and friendship, but only the continual grasping calculation of something to be got from men and things as they served a more or less transient need. The convenience of a utensil would be the highest form of praise. Hobbes has already described this state and called it 'the Natural Condition of Mankind'. 'No Arts, no Letters, no Society; and which is worst of all, continual fear and danger of violent death'. It would be a life 'solitary' for certain: whether also 'poor, nasty, brutish, and short' might depend partly on circumstances.

II AFFECTION AND THOUGHT

But of course desire is not the whole of life. In man's mind, even at its most primitive, there is another principle at work, a principle which counteracts the fierce abstractions of desire and contains the germ of a more adequate grasp of reality. The materials which the senses furnish are in fact submitted to other developments, in which individuality is not sacrificed but remains central. And it is on this principle, in the last resort, that all the higher developments of human nature depend.

It is easy enough, even at the lowest levels of life, to point to phenomena for which desire does not account, which must therefore be supposed to be manifestations of another principle; and on analysis these phenomena show a precisely opposite tendency which makes this rival principle the fit complement of desire. This principle I will call affection, using the word in the current sense, as the substantive corresponding to the adjective 'affectionate'. It is to be seen at work, I suggest, in any act or activity for which a particular thing or person has its own peculiar significance and is irreplaceable by another particular of the same kind. Its application must not be confined to persons, though in personal relations it finds no doubt its fullest and most characteristic expression. Inanimate things also commonly acquire a value of their own: they come to be incorporated into a man's life as intimate ingredients of it, endlessly provocative of fruitful activity. A town or a countryside, a house and garden, a familiar street, a favourite chair or pen—these and other such particular things acquire for a particular individual a uniquely stimulating character, which is quite independent of any comparison with other individuals of the same general type, and makes them strictly irreplaceable. This is the true intimate meaning of property, that natural property to which the French Revolution declared man's inalienable right—things that are one's own as one's self is one's own. The relation is merely enriched and further complicated when the object of affection is a living being, capable of answering activity by activity and affection by affection. Neither love nor hatred can be reduced to manifestations of desire; and, though desire here also plays its part, the more positive values of family life and of social life generally depend mainly without doubt on personal affection. And indeed it seems evident that character and personality are so dependent on this principle of affection, that if we suppose it lacking or wholly unsatisfied, they would not exist, and if we suppose it weakened they are weakened with it. Mere desire is as ruthless and impersonal as an earthquake or any other overwhelming natural force.

Thought, which is the creature of human interest, responds to affection as it responded to desire. In obedience to desire, as we saw, it abstracts and generalizes. In response to affection thought dwells on each observed particular, grouping and uniting them, not by classification, as they exemplify certain types, but by the principle of individuality, so that they are seen to build up a relatively independent and self-contained system, which retains in some sense a single character through all its successive phases. Nothing is omitted or discounted, but some features are felt as more characteristic than others; as in all systems, there is subordination, which gives ample opportunity for doubts and hesitations, as for differences of interpretation. If the observer will think individually at all, he must needs frame his own hypothesis, form his own view of the character observed; and this will be done by forcing a certain emphasis and rhythm upon the various appearances. His hypothesis will be continuously tested in its continuous effort to digest the appearances; it will insensibly modify and correct itself, deepen and enrich itself, as time goes on. There will not as a rule be any startling changes or turning points in this development. A man's growing knowledge of his friend or of his country does not proceed by revolutionary discoveries—such surprises as occur are apt to seem much less surprising in retrospect—but cumulatively, by constant watchfulness and unending readiness to learn more. It is an account which in the nature of the case must never be considered closed, and there can be no finality of judgment. Progress is marked only by gradually increasing understanding, by greater confidence in interpretation and prediction; but doubt is never quite excluded, and an absolute of 'knowledge' is not even conceivable.

It seems also to be the case that in the attitude of affection the observer's own position and his relation to the observed belong to the fundamental data of thought, as they do not when thought is actualized by desire. This may look like a paradox, since the desirous act is very naturally described as an act in which the agent takes something for himself, and the typical act of affection is apt to be thought of as one in which the agent gives something away. But the direct opposition already formulated between the concreteness of the one attitude and the abstractness of the other will be readily seen to entail this as a consequence. In the act of desire a *hungry person* seeks *food*; names and personalities are of as little importance on the one side as on the other. Indeed to name or otherwise individualize the thing eaten would be to make it repulsive and almost impossible to eat. The act would approximate at once to cannibalism. And you cannot thus denature one term in a relation and leave the other unaffected. Common sense may say that John Smith is eating his dinner; but it is not really John Smith that eats, and the food that will presently go to form his body is not really his. But into the relations established by affection he enters whole and entire with all his peculiarities of status and character. The things and persons bound to him by affection—his home, his wife and children, his friends, his country—these are really his. The whole series of relations depends essentially on his unique position in the scheme of things, and constitute, if not his personality, at least what we may call, by misusing a legal term, his personality. The principle of affection creates relations of individuals in respect of their individuality. If desire makes man a vagrant and a spendthrift, by his affections he is a miser and a stay-at-home.

Since both principles are continuously and simultaneously operative in human nature, it is very natural that they should be often confused and mistaken for one another. Desire is in fact commonly complicated by the intrusion of affection and affection similarly by that of desire. In action of any considerable degree of elaboration it will usually be difficult to distinguish precisely the part played by each principle. The instances of the tie of affection already given provide ample illustration of the contamination of affection by desire. The intimate personal tie of property for instance comes to be confused with, or even completely absorbed in, the wholly impersonal desirous category of wealth. It is then reckoned in terms of money, which is the mere abstract potentiality of possession, and, by reason of its absolute transferability and its complete indifference to individuals in every sense, has been rightly taken, since the days of Plato, as the most perfect symbol of generalized desire. Similarly, the natural and proper attachment of each of us to the place where he was born and brought up, to the familiar uses of his home and kindred, turns into an aggressive assertion of the superiority of these to others, expressed in action as the attempt to enrich and aggrandize these at the expense of others. This conversion is so common and superficially at least so complete, that many thinkers argue that there is nothing in patriotism but competitive desire. But the most inexhaustible field for the mixture and confusion of these principles in fact, fancy, and fiction is the relation between men and women. Here the cynic sees nothing but desire and the romantic only affection. The ideal of marriage requires the operation of both principles, desire being confined and canalized by affection.

In all these three cases—property, patriotism, and the intimacy of the sexes—there have been found purists who have condemned the whole relation, as the sign or source of the corruption of human nature. But however different they may be in many other respects, they are all alike in this, that they all spring from normal and ineradicable human tendencies, and each in its development becomes a field of battle on which the two principles we are discussing fight it out together. In this struggle they become confused. Love and lust, property and wealth, loyalty and jingoism, intermingle in fact and in men's thoughts; and the condemnation of the perversion is allowed to discredit the whole relation. But however intricate the interplay of the two principles may be, surely all these situations are much elucidated when it is recognized that in each there are these two opposed and independent tendencies at issue, producing in their conflict fundamental problems of human life and society.

My point then is that, however far back we go into the origins of man, and however far forward we follow his development, we shall never be able to give a credible explanation of his behaviour by means of the single principle of desire, even if we lend it the assistance of its child, purpose. We shall always need at least one other principle. And I have argued that the field is in general covered if we supplement desire by affection; if, as complement to the attitude in which things are significant only in their general character, we recognize an attitude in which things are individually significant. If unregulated human intercourse is more decent and tolerable than Hobbes suggested, that is because he wilfully and paradoxically composed his man of desire alone; the same passion, he said, was called desire when its object was absent and love when it was present.

We have only to introduce affection into the picture—i.e. to insist that love is different in kind from desire—to set some limit to competition and bring some order into social relations. For affection makes each man and home and place an individual centre different from every other, and when thus fixed by affection they are in certain important respects removed from competition. The basis of order, and so ultimately of justice, is that things and persons should have each its assured place.

III   ILLUSTRATIONS

I will now try to indicate shortly some applications of which the theme I have been developing seems to admit. It is commonly said—and surely with evident truth—that a man's knowledge of persons depends on the width and depth of his affections more than on anything else. The truth of this is only seen the more clearly if some necessary qualifications and explanations are added. There is a knowledge of persons which does not depend on affection—such a knowledge as might be shown by a rather inhuman despot, by a military officer or sergeant-major, by the foreman or manager of a great business, in whose hands a multitude of appointments lay. Such a ruler or official might show great knowledge of men in the sense that he had an unerring instinct for putting the square peg in the square hole and the round peg in the round hole; he might be an expert in finding the job for the man; and he might yet have little interest in the men as individuals and little knowledge of them in that sense. The thought implicit in his particular decisions would be a thought which arranged men in classes and allowed complete interchangeability within each class; in the fashion characteristic, as we have seen, of thought when employed in the service of desire. Knowledge of men, when credited to public officials, often means no more than this; and if so, clearly it is no proof of affection. But if by knowledge of persons is meant a real understanding of their thoughts and actions, so that wishes can be anticipated and unexpressed intentions carried out, if in short is meant contact with individuals in their individuality, then it seems that affection is the only key. Not that affection suffices by itself. Clearly it does not; but, in proportion as affection is lacking, judgment is insecure and uncertain.

This principle may have no clear application in the field of science, which is a world, as we know, of classes and abstractions, but it has very obvious applications in history and biography, which, however scientific they may claim to be, are yet obliged by their very nature to attempt a vision of the individuality of an individual object. It is evident that the work of a historian demands a width of sympathy and imagination of which few men are capable; and perhaps if any historian ever succeeds in showing that he has not set himself an impossible task, it is because knowledge tends to increase and expand the affection which made it possible. And, of course, most so-called historical writing is not history, but only a memorandum of data for a history that may one day be written. Similarly a real biography in which life is more than a mere word, is the rarest of things, and the few examples are, like Boswell's *Johnson*, obviously tributes of affection.

The importance of affection is quite as fundamental in the field of aesthetic appreciation. In art and literature we all have our likes and dislikes; and much confusion arises from our attempts to justify these by the principles of the art in question. These judgments are often more complicated than they appear to be, and genuinely aesthetic elements may be contained in them; but in general a dislike signifies failure to make effective contact and constitutes a disqualification for judging. It is at least doubtful whether an honest critic should speak at all except where his affections are engaged; but here, as in history and biography, there are formal and external relations which can be established by mere honest observations and analysis. That such analysis, necessarily conducted in general terms, results in a mere classification, and not in an understanding of the work in its individuality is, I think, obvious. It does not follow that the analysis is not worth making, nor even that it may not contribute something to the aesthetic appreciation, which is the understanding of the work in its individuality. What I am saying is that this appreciation, unlike the analysis, is impossible without affection or liking; and I suggest that this fact explains the fundamental difficulty which confronts the composer of any general history of art or literature. The limits of the possible extension of the affections are soon reached; and therefore the historian of art, unless his mind be of heroic cast, must either operate within a very narrow range or confine his work for most of its course to the scientific and classificatory plane.

In morality the importance of affection will probably be readily conceded. It will be agreed that the right attitude to other persons within the scope of one's action is to treat them as persons, as existing in their own right, rather than as instruments of desire or as particular instances of a class (child, shopkeeper, servant, etc.). That is the sense of Kant's injunction to treat persons as ends in themselves, not merely as means. It will also be agreed that affection creates this attitude to persons. But since we are by no means free to choose with whom we shall associate, a difficulty arises here, which Kant points out. 'Affection', he says, 'cannot be commanded'. Therefore when we are told to love our neighbour, and even our enemy, we must suppose love, 'practical' and not love 'pathological'—a will, not an emotion—to be intended. Kant's phrase, 'a love seated in the will, not in the bias of sentiment', may seem a mere evasion of the difficulty, since it may well be doubted whether the strongest will can extract from a temperamental aversion the fruits of genuine affection. But the difficulty must be put aside here, with the reminder that we have not asserted, and do not wish to assert, that in any sphere affection by itself suffices, only that it supplies the indispensable foundation.

Finally, since philosophy cannot rest content with a conception of knowledge which excludes the individual altogether, as that of science does, it seems that affection must be said to be essential also to knowledge. If we do not wish reality to become an ultimate abstraction, a sort of class of classes, we must suppose that it is within the power of metaphysics to restore individuality to its place in the final account, and in so doing to justify as knowledge the grasp of the changing situation by which man lives, as well as those offshoots from it which are given over to the specialists—not merely the abstractions of man's science and mathematics, but also his achievements or aspirations in history and biography, in art and literature, in religion, in the knowledge of particular men and things and places. The attribution of omniscience to God is common in religious writing; but there is one text that has impressed itself upon men's imagination beyond all others: 'Are not two sparrows sold for a farthing? and one of them shall not fall to the ground without your Father. But the very hairs of your head are all numbered'. The text owes its special appeal to the fact that it suggests at the same time infinite knowledge and infinite love.

The general thesis of the paper is that, if human behaviour is seen as due to the interaction of thought and desire, a one-sided and incorrect picture necessarily results, because desire accounts only for an interest in a certain *kind* of thing and excludes direct interest in individuals. It is argued that a supplementary principle, called affection, must be invoked to account for interest in individuals, and that this principle is a fundamental condition of all man's higher activities.

Such terms as desire, thought, affection, are abstractions, and are inevitably to some extent arbitrary. They are devices by which reflective analysis tries to reduce to order the complicated phenomena of conduct. No finality should ever be claimed for any such classification. Probably the phenomena are best understood if they are analysed in as many different ways as possible. But it is necessary to demand that a classification shall give some guarantee of its own completeness; and in this respect there is room for legitimate objection to many classifications of popular and professional psychology. Nothing turns in this paper on the question whether what I have called 'thought' and 'desire' (keeping as near as possible to popular usage) are products of the best or most convenient division. It suffices that these, or related, terms are in common use. What I suggest is that if these abstractions are made, they must be supplemented by a third which I call affection.

The thesis then is that the behaviour of a man, his total activity or occupation in any moment of being, cannot be truthfully expressed by means of the terms 'desire' and 'thought' alone, but can be truthfully expressed by means of the trio, desire—affection—thought.

This means that in man, as accounting for his behaviour, we are asked to postulate at any moment:

(1) A predisposition to action called desire—i.e. a readiness to undertake elaborate series of movements, which, however much they may differ in detail, conform to a general type in their result and in their relation to the normal processes of the human organism.

(2) A capacity to take in the general features of the situation, including ultimately the desire itself. This capacity may be called generally Thought.

(3) The third factor which I wish to introduce is to be supposed so far to be on the same plane with desire, that it, like desire, is a precondition of thought. It stimulates, guides, and limits thought as desire does; and primitive thought will be wholly unaware of this control by affection just as it is unaware of its control by desire. More highly developed thought will discover these limitations and will be able partly, though never wholly, to overcome them. Thus affection is a predisposition, like desire.

Unlike the fundamental desires (instincts), however, it is not a predisposition common to the species, but one personal to the individual. It ties him to *his* parents, friends, home, etc., which are only shared by accident with others. Again, while each appetite has its organs with biologically fixed uses, affection has no organ and no specific mode of action. It is wholly unspecialized in its expression. The

elements in behaviour which are characteristic of the affectionate person in relation to the object of affection are such
as these; the attempt to be with the object as much as
possible; the tendency to give action continual reference to
the object, especially to help and not hinder it, to improve
and look after it, and so on.

Here is an instance. A little girl of my acquaintance
(aged six) acquired a bicycle by gift from another little girl
who had outgrown it. When she knew that she was to have
it, but before it came, she addressed to this bicycle these
lines:

> O beautiful bike, I love you so:
> It is so nice to see you go.
> I will wash you and clean you and take
>     you home—
> O beautiful bike, will you come?

In the background, no doubt, was the desire for a bicycle.
If this gift had fallen through, another ideal bicycle would
very likely have taken its place. But the poem breathes pure
affection—the delight in contemplating the characteristic
motions of the beloved object, the care for it, the absorption
in the life of the lover. The prey has become the charge:
desire has been domesticated by affection.

# 3

# *Moral Values*

## I

A study of moral values is a study of the values relevant to character and conduct. Since conduct consists of actions (including refusals to act) and character is exhibited in and inferred from actions, the phrase 'values relevant to actions' would perhaps suffice. The term 'values' needs little amplification. But it is necessary to observe that there are on the face of it two sets of values relevant to actions, namely, (1) those which actions themselves possess, so that we differentiate them as good and bad actions—a differentiation which may be made by a spectator in regard to a process in which he himself takes no part; (2) those asserted implicitly by an agent in his action considered as an interference with the course of events. In the most obvious and typical cases this second set of values attach themselves, not to actions, but to the environment of action as modifiable by it; in particular, to states or events which action may help to maintain or bring about. Thus the act of tidying a room implies a preference under the given circumstances for a tidy rather than an untidy room. Whether, and if so in what sense, a value of the first classs, i.e. the goodness or badness of an action, can serve as a value of the second class, i.e. as a determinant of intelligent choice or purpose, is a disputed question. Clearly a human being, in virtue of his self-consciousness, is able to become the spectator of himself; and before engaging in action, or while engaged upon it, he may ask himself how the action itself should be valued or judged. He thus becomes the judge in imagination of himself, and it seems natural to suppose that the result of this intellectual experiment may be to lead him to modify or discontinue the line of action projected or initiated. If so, the value implied in his discontinuance or modified continuation will be in part at least a value of the first class which determines action and thus serves as a value of the second class.

That such an imaginative self-judgment plays an important, if not essential, part in what we call morality, most moralists, ancient and modern, who are not pure utilitarians or hedonists, have explicitly or implicitly maintained; and I myself am disposed to agree with them in this. Only I do not think it explains quite as much as some of them thought it explained, and I have to admit that there are serious difficulties which can only be circumvented by very cautious and careful statement. The chief difficulty arises from the fact that the essence of action seems to be the valuations implied in it, i.e. the main ground for favourable valuation of an action (for asserting value [1]) is full acceptance of the valuations of the second class which the action seems to presuppose in the agent. In more ordinary terms, an action to be reckoned good must exhibit sound preferences. For instance, an action which seems to imply a preference for the unhappiness of others is so far bad, and an action which implies a preference for their happiness is so far good. Now suppose a man finds himself engaged in a course of action which, if continued (as he discovers by imaginative self-judgment), would be open to the former interpretation, and stigmatized as cruel. Suppose that, on becoming aware of this, he modifies his action, so that it is not open to this interpretation. What has happened? Clearly he will be entitled to escape the blame which attaches to callousness or cruelty; but he does not seem to be entitled to the praise which is accorded to benevolence, i.e. the active preference for the happiness of others. It cannot be supposed that the reflection that the projected act would be judged by an impartial spectator to be cruel or callous will of itself create a *direct* motive to an action of opposite tendency. There is therefore no real benevolence in the amended course of action, no preference for the happiness of others in itself. What is operative is a preference for a line of action which will not involve him in self-condemnation.

Though conscience is often said to be the guide of life, its operations (so far as they are investigated at all) are commonly conceived after the foregoing model. 'Thus conscience doth make cowards of us all.' But clearly the conscience which makes men cowards is rather a censor than a guide. Its decrees form a kind of criminal law; it intervenes to deter and punish; and the very nature of its action implies a better state in which it would be reduced to inactivity by the removal of all grounds for interference. In the perfectly healthy will conscience is in abeyance, as the criminal law will disappear from sight in a perfectly healthy community. But if this is so, then either conscience is not of the essence of morality, or there is a goal beyond morality on which morality depends for its meaning. Classical Greek thought argued cogently that justice cannot be supposed to reside in the action of the judge who directs the restoration of the social order where it has been disturbed; that would make its existence dependent on the presence of defect and disorder; the positive value must lie in the order itself which the action corrected by the judge disturbs. So here, if the action of conscience is correctly typified by the above example, it must surely be conceded that the intervention of conscience derives its value from a further good in whose interest it intervenes; its action is instrumental merely and conditioned by the presence of defect. Or, recurring to the two classes of values, the same point may be put thus: It would seem that the intrusion of values of the first class into the determination of action—i.e. their appearance among values of the second class—cannot be of the essence of morality, unless morality is merely a second best. For this intrusion implies in its very nature an ideal in which the values implicit in action are perfectly acceptable to an impartial observer, which means, as we have seen, that values of the first class do not appear among them.

## II

I propose now to undertake an analysis of action with a view to throwing further light on the problem just stated. An action is essentially an interference by a person with the course of events, and its implications may be followed in two directions—not in complete independence of one another—into the personality of the agent on the one hand and into the environment affected on the other. Thus an action may be valued in two ways: (1) in respect of its contribution to the course of events, (2) in respect of the mind or character shown in it. Since events are more directly observable and more easily analysed than characters, the first valuation is the more easily made, and until some progress has been made with it, the second valuation is in fact impossible. But it is incontestable that a valuation of an act in respect of its contribution to the course of events is far from a complete valuation of it. It may be possible under favourable conditions to determine accurately the kind and degree of contribution which a given action—the saying of certain words or the application of remedies to a wound—has made to a known relatively simple issue, e.g. the resignation of a minister, the survival of a wounded soldier; but if the whole is really to be interpreted as action, and not as a mere concatenation of movements, it must be seen finally as the activity or self-expression of a human personality. For this purpose the results must be reformulated as intentions, and at once a doubt arises how far the results actually accruing can be taken to correspond with the results anticipated by the agent at the time of the act, perhaps even how far the knowledge available at the time of action would have enabled anyone to foretell the issue. It is therefore a very paradoxical view of the Utilitarians that the valuation of action proceeds (or should proceed) only by reckoning results; but even they admit that there are these two lines of judgement which may give rise to divergent estimates; only

they prefer to regard the second kind of valuation as a valuation of the agent rather than of the act, and argue that this
valuation of the agent depends itself ultimately on results,
since to call him good is to recognize him as capable of
making great contributions to human welfare. It seems
clear that a full understanding of action must pursue both
sets of implications, and that the distinction between valuation of the agent and valuation of the act cannot in this sense
be upheld. It also seems clear that the moral philosopher, in
his capacity as moral philosopher, is not occupied in reform-
ing the world, but in trying to understand what moral value
is, and therefore that he is not interested in the contribution
of action to the course of events for its own sake at all, but
only as evidence of the mind and will which the agent
expressed in the act. The second valuation is the one in
which he is interested, and in the first only incidentally as
throwing light upon it.

So far we have adopted the point of view of the spectator
of an action, who can follow it in two directions, to its
source in the character of the agent and to its issue in the
welter of events. If we now adopt the point of view of the
agent himself, we shall find a parallel, but somewhat
modified dualism. He will justify his actions, if they are
questioned, mainly in terms of the external series: 'this is
done in order to make that possible', and so on; but the
explanation will depend for its plausibility, at least as often
as not, on the fact that the result to which the action leads
represents something that the agent likes or desires. Thus
the constructive effort which is his action is found to be
expressive of desire or liking. He will also observe, if he
observes his own behaviour at all closely, an amount of
detail in it, which is purely expressive in its character. I do
not mean that the movements in question have no effect on
his environment; only that they appear to be made without
any reference to their possible effects on it. A man will
speak loud because the person he is speaking to is deaf and
because he likes to be heard; but he may also speak loud
because he is angry, or because it is his habit so to speak. A

wounded man will cry out, and his cries may actually bring people to help him; but it was not with that object that he cried. Every one has his tricks of speech and movement which, though they may on occasion be used for certain ends, exist and persist independently of purpose and even to its prejudice. Actions, then, regarded from the point of view of the agent, have a dual character, as expressive on the one hand and constructive on the other. In the one view they are regarded as contributions to the flow of events and as justified by what occurs there; in the other they are seen to be explained, if not justified, by some state or attitude of the agent himself. It is in principle the same dualism as before; but the agent tends to regard action rather in its constructive aspect, the spectator rather on its expressive side. Character and motive bulk much more largely in our judgments of other people than in our own decisions.

Action is not born rational, and on the basis so far offered it is not easy to see how it should ever become rational. On every side it seems to run back into some inexplicable personal caprice. As expressive it refers us to desires, emotions, instincts, habits, likings, affections—a motley crowd into which it will be convenient not to enquire further—and generally to a personal idiosyncrasy, which in practice earns a chuckle of delighted recognition when the personality is one we like, and a snort of disgust when it is one we dislike. And on the other, the constructive plane, as formative of events, it only maintains its apparent reasonableness so long as we forget that the issues to which it works are ends dictated by this same idiosyncrasy, referring us equally to the surd of psychical fact. The irrational preferences in which action is born are presuppositions of the apparently rational preferences in which its maturity finds expression; the development is merely in the direction of increased persistence and tenacity in the pursuit of an arbitrary end.

But though action is not born rational, it strives to become rational; it tries to rationalize itself, i.e. to become such that it can justify itself completely to itself and to others. Moral theorists have usually attempted to exhibit morality as part of the struggle towards rationalization or as its goal. The form under which we first find ourselves naturally impelled to rationalize action is that of purpose, which involves an analysis into means and end; and the simplest conception of morality (the special value which attaches to action as such) is that of complete success in this endeavour. Good action is that which is fully and completely rational, which means action that can exhibit itself as the pursuit of the right end by the right means.

This simple and obvious scheme breaks down completely on analysis—first, because of its own inherent weakness: action cannot be completely rationalized on these lines at all; secondly, by its inability to account for our actual moral judgements, because the rationalization of action on these lines, so far as it can be carried out, does not necessarily mean the achievement of good action.

To see how it breaks down, let us dismiss all question as to means, supposing them in every case beyond criticism, and concentrate on ends. We find a number of different things—states or relations or events—which the various actions are said to be justified by their tendency to produce; products of action for which the actions which generate them are valued. If these are left a mere multiplicity, in no relation to one another, the adoption of a given end in a given situation remains a mere irrational caprice. They have therefore to be brought in some way into a unity, either by being exhibited as some sort of system, or by being represented as contributing to a single ultimate product or end on which they all converge. But no such ultimate end can be found: if there is a 'far off divine event to which the whole creation moves', man has not found it; and the system of all goods, though it may exist and operate unconsciously in human action, escapes definition and description, and must therefore fail to serve as the recognized justification of human action. Thus action refuses to be rationalized because ends refuse to form a unity. The choice of ends is not in practice justified by reference to an

57

ultimate end, but rather by common consent and usage. No aim, it is assumed, is unreasonable which all men or most men adopt.

Further, such justification of action, whether complete or incomplete, is not a moral justification of action. The general principle of its argument is that the end justifies the means; and morality refuses to accept this principle. It insists on questioning means which can be shown to be the best within reach to a perfectly reasonable or generally accepted end. The demand of morality enters not as a last clarification of the nexus of means and end, nor as an illumination of the mutual relations of our ends which reduces all to system and makes the way quite straight and plain, but as an additional complication, something impinging on these purposes from without, disturbing and hampering their execution. All attempts to reduce the apparent conflict to harmony, by representing the demand of morality as the call of a more distant or more real end, break down, and must break down, because the conflict is of the essence of the matter, and because in accepting such demands no specific product can be found to which men's effort is directed. A purpose is judged by its fruits, and claims no other test. Morality has no special fruit of its own, and the issue of the actions in which it is specially engaged is indistinguishable to the closest inspection from those in which it is not. The goodness of a good man does not depend on this, that he has a different end from a bad man, or a clearer view of the same end, or a single end where he has many. One or more of these superiorities he may well possess, but these by themselves do not constitute moral eminence. His distinctive gift and power must be sought elsewhere.

### III

In the foregoing I have taken the term purpose as appropriate to the outward and forward looking attitude of a man who is trying to manipulate the elements of a situation so as to bring something about. It represents, then, concentration on results, and the future reference is inevitable.

This interpretation is natural if action is regarded in its constructive aspect. The systematization of purpose so regarded is necessarily an attempt to represent each act as a contribution to a single great structure which is being built up piecemeal, some vision of the structure as a whole controlling each addition to it. But the attempt may also be made to co-ordinate action under its expressive aspect, with reference to its source in personality; and from this angle the future reference may seem less obvious—or at least less central—and a rather different interpretation of purpose may be possible. The progress of action towards rationalization, on this interpretation, will be from the random and disconnected expressions of desire and impulse, in which the man is one-sidedly active, in the direction of an ideal in which every act is the expression of a unified and harmonious personality identifying itself wholly with the act. This view, stated thus in general terms, is immediately attractive, partly because it brings us back to the obviously fundamental ground of character, partly because our own familiar experience of life convinces us that some such internal harmony is characteristic of men who have achieved real goodness. But it is necessary to look the idea more closely in the face than that, and on closer inspection a number of things seem plain.

First, if this idea is to have any precision, the most fundamental requirement is a clear idea of the multiplicity out of which purpose and character emerge and of the unity or harmony into which they grow or try to grow. The names of Plato and Bishop Butler come to mind at once as thinkers who have tried this method of approach; but both attempts may well be judged defective in the detail of their account. Neither of them wrestles very seriously with the primaeval multitude of impulses or 'particular propensions', and neither of them succeeds in establishing any positive relation between the controlling power (philosophy in Plato, conscience in Butler) and the multitude controlled; so that the organization resembles rather a dictatorship than a system or harmony, and the fundamental problem remains unsolved—as so often in a dictatorship—whence does the dictator draw the strength to maintain his position.

Secondly, it is essential to clear up the relation between this internal order, from which as source good action proceeds, and the external efficacies in which it issues. The terminology of means and end has been used to express the relation, but it is plainly inadequate for the purpose. Nothing is properly called an end which is not causally connected with changes directly initiated in the action. But if the causal implications of these changes are followed out, they will no doubt in the long run at one point or another return upon the agent as external forces influencing his condition and behaviour; but the self influenced must be a future self, not the actual self expressed in the action. And the explanation wanted is that of the relation between the present self and its issue in act. The self is commonly thought of as *determining* the act. This present self cannot be at once the determinant and part of that which is determined, at once cause and effect. Being cause, it cannot be effect, and not being effect it cannot be the end of action. If we suppose (as seems reasonable) that this internal order is such that it can only be generated and expressed in and through action, the terminology of means and end is plainly inappropriate to the relation between it and the action in which it is expressed.

The painter's gift is such as can be expressed only in pictures. If we are asked to apply means and end here, we are puzzled. Is the existence of the painter justified by that of the picture, or the existence of the picture by that of the painter, or are both means to the existence of art? These questions are probably not worth answering; but if a choice had to be made between the alternatives offered, we should be safest in choosing the first. It is certainly true, though it may not be a very important truth, that painters continue to exist because pictures are wanted. It is also true, and probably a much more important truth, that pictures express their makers; further, you can say without absurdity that the picture is what it is because the painter is what he is; but there is no causal sequence here as in the former case. The demand for pictures might exist for a time unsatisfied, but what is there expressed could not be unexpressed except in the sense that the picture might not exist. The painter's skill and vision and their expression are both to be found, so far as they can be distinguished, within the work of art. The causal relation, which by a convenient modern restriction has come to involve temporal sequence, is therefore excluded, and with it the terminology of means and end. The relation is between co-existents. Of course there is also the fact that the artist is not devoid of foresight and prudence, and that one of the considerations that will influence his production will be the development and maintenance of his artistic gift. He may, e.g. attempt what is for him a quite novel subject or treatment with the deliberate idea of widening his range. So far as such considerations operate, there will be a genuine future reference, and so far the terminology of means and end will be appropriate. But this is accidental, not essential; on these lines only a very partial and as it were external account of the works he actually produces can be given.

With the necessary changes all this can be transferred to the moral agent, conceived (as we are now conceiving him) as expressing a disciplined and ordered personality in action. For him also any reference to a future state of himself, to the further maintenance and development of his internal order and discipline, will be accidental, not essential—forced upon him from time to time because circumstances happen to be such as to threaten future disturbance. The act and the character shown in it are coexistents, not antecedent and consequent; and means and end, cause and effect are equally inappropriate to their relation. Where occasionally these terms are appropriate, they apply not to a relation between character and act, but to a relation between a present and a future character-act complex.

Thirdly, however true it may be that the ordered unity of character described represents the finest achievement of humanity and the highest moral value, it is impossible to find in the conception of such a unity a full and sufficient ground for the actual practical decisions which a person possessing it would take. It may be granted that in every decision he will maintain and develop this unity, and from time to time some element in his decisions may be directly due to his determination to develop and maintain it, but in general the detail of his actions has to be supplied from elsewhere. Until this detail is in some way supplied he can have no formed purpose or intention whatever; therefore he is not rightly described as having an end. End and means are correlatives like form and matter, and the convenience of the analysis by which we distinguish them must not be allowed to make us suppose them separable. Ends exist only in means chosen for their sake, as form exists only in matter, though form and end, being universals, are not confined to this or that particular vehicle. There is no preliminary stage of mere thought, in which an end is conceived and the possible means to its realization explored, followed by a stage of mere action, in which the plan is carried out. The active life does not cease while we think, and our thought is at its most intense while we act. The process is not from abstract to concrete, from the thought of a pleasure to the fact of enjoyment. An oak-tree does not begin with the thought of an oak, but with an acorn, which is a germinal oak, and similarly a full-grown manifestation of the human will has its antecedent in half-grown and germinal predecessors of the same kind. The early stages in the development of purpose are all of the nature of action, though they may give no indication of their existence to an external observer.

By sense and thought man is kept in continuous touch with the development of the situation in which he maintains himself; his mind reaches before and after, and without conscious effort he senses the direction of events; on the basis of what is present he is always preparing himself for what may come. He is always reviewing and revising his dispositions, putting one tool away and taking up another, changing his own attitude and posture; and every act is part anticipation. Watch any activity which is mainly physical in its expression, and the description is easily verified. The skilled tennis player moves smoothly from his stroke to the place where the return may be expected and assumes the position of readiness to meet it. His end or aim is not embodied in a preconceived plan which he carries out according to specification; it is rather something that may be detected in the whole series of movements as a control and determinant of direction, something also that may be distinguished analytically from them as form from matter, essence from accident. The detail of expression depends on circumstance. Given the persistent aim and tendency, at any moment a variation in the opponent's behaviour would have dictated a variation in the game developed to meet them.

Now a tennis player, like other people, may be supposed to have various ends in playing tennis, many of them perfectly compatible with one another. He may want exercise or distinction or victory; he may be concerned to recommend himself to a particular person, or for a particular appointment, or to win a particular prize. Let us suppose that in the given case all such concerns are absent or quite subordinate, and that his main preoccupation is to express and maintain his own skill at the game. His attitude then will be precisely similar to the moral attitude with which we are concerned—that which takes as ultimate a certain harmony and unity of character. All ends, I have said, are formal, in that they determine the general nature of what is done, but not its detail. But if there are degrees of formality, this preoccupation must be adjudged more formal still. For it does not determine what is to be done at all—not even in its most general outline: it merely determines that if certain things are done (if, e.g. tennis is played), they shall be done in a certain way (i.e. in a manner worthy of the player's skill). Morality, however, unlike tennis, is coextensive with action, and therefore with life. Hence a similar formal requirement framed in the name of morality loses this hypothetical character, and becomes a quite general demand that whatever is done shall be done in a certain way. In both cases (tennis and morality) I suggest that submission to such a requirement is not properly described as the adoption or prosecution of an end: it is a requirement generally compatible with any end and occasionally found in conflict with all; and, further, that action considered as conformed to such demands is better not described as purposive, since it is convenient to restrict purpose to the attitude of concentration on ends. But if you choose to extend the term purpose to include all open-eyed activity, then you will be justified in calling art and morality purposive, and you will have to invent another word to represent concentration on ends.

We have now arrived by a rather tortuous path at the suggestion that the moral demand is a demand that whatever is done shall be done in a certain way. Vague as this formula at present is, I want to consider it seriously and on its own merits. But first let me make a remark arising from my use of the word hypothetical above. It may be supposed that when I use hypothetical of the demand of skill and refuse to use it of the demand of morality, I am introducing a well-known Kantian distinction and preparing the way for the categorical imperative. Well, it would perhaps be no bad thing if our argument brought us back to Kant; but I feel bound to point out that it has not so far done so. My contrast was between a restricted and an unrestricted reference, between something universally applicable and something which applies only in a special region. The character of the demand, where it happens to be in place, is not affected by this distinction. To the tennis player engaged in his game, to the artist at work upon his art, the demand of his skill for its maintenance and due expression is as categorical as any demand can be: there is nothing conditional about it. As it operates, it controls and limits the use of skill in ways which the ends in view alone fail to explain, and we call it the artist's self-respect, or sometimes the artistic conscience. The last is a good name for it, for it is, as we shall now see, the principle which in that limited but autonomous sphere plays the part which in life as a whole is played by the moral principle. It does not determine the work to be done, but it lays down conditions negative and positive as to its doing.

Action, as I said, strives to become rational and self-justifying. In its constructive aspect, ordered under the notion of purpose, it can achieve a certain unity, but not that final and satisfying unity which it desires. We have here the suggestion of another principle of unity—not a rival, I think, but an ally—which may tie some of the loose ends and give a general continuity to the practical life.

### IV

Let us go back for a moment to our tennis player. He is playing a game; and into the origination and conduct of the game all sorts of motives may enter each emphasizing some particular element in the complex activity and some particular line of future continuation, all, however, depending on the established convention that he is trying to beat his opponent. This convention dictates one standing purpose or aim which he must maintain throughout; and the other motives derived from probable consequences of the activity presuppose this standing purpose and rather strengthen than weaken it. (Of course he might have reasons for wishing not to beat his opponent, but such a motive would be an interference with the game, and so far as effective would introduce an element of deceit and pretence into his action.) Distinct in kind from all these motives and calculations, but also capable of modifying the player's behaviour, is the player's tennis conscience. If he is to play tennis, he will play tennis, not pat-ball. This determination of his will not normally interfere with any projects that he may have built upon the game. The more truly he plays tennis, the better he plays; the better he plays, the more likely he is to win the game, to get his exercise, etc. Normally there is perfect harmony; but occasionally, exceptionally, there is trouble. The player finds himself indignantly turning away from tactics which would bring certain victory—why? Because, he would probably say, they are not his idea of tennis. Now, considered with reference to victory or any other end pursued in the game, this diversion necessarily appears as a limitation of the means by which they may be secured. The end is not denied, but its ability to justify these means is denied. Thus it is an insistence that an act shall be done in a certain way, a specification of conditions positive and negative. It makes its presence felt as limiting the activity, just as the law of the land enters occasionally as a limit and determinant into the lives of its citizens.

This is how it inevitably appears to one concentrated on the issue and the result. But what is it? and what is its title to interfere? We have already seen what it is and we have already vindicated its title. The man is actually playing tennis, and the basis of the interference is simply the recognition that this is what he is doing, and the demand, naturally associated with it, that he shall really and truly do it. There could be no simpler or more fundamental consideration. For though as an explicit factor in decision the conception of tennis-playing may be an occasional and intermittent visitor, yet no proof or apology is required surely for the thesis that this conception is really the basis and foundation on which all the rest is built. This is the root from which the fruits to which our purposes are directed spring; and if the root is poisoned or cut away, the fruits will soon fail and wither. It is not truly our purposes that are interfered with; they are at best intermittent, dependent on circumstance and opportunity. It is the activity that is the constant factor and continuing form, and it is this that occasionally is endangered by the material in which it finds embodiment. On such occasions the activity asserts itself in self-defence against the danger of self-mutilation or suicide under pressure of events.

What I wish to maintain is that the basis of moral judgment and the root of moral values is a similar but quite general conception of will and action as a continuing form finding its changing embodiment in the changing situations of life; that such a conception is at the foundation of all effort and every purpose, however rare may be the proofs it gives of its existence in the familiar form of scruples of conscience or of exactions in the name of duty which can be traced to no other source. Here alone, I would argue, is the unity we were seeking to be found—so much unity, at least, as is to be reached by a finite being in his finitude. It cannot be found, as we have seen, in any end; nor can it be found at any point in the changing states of the self or by any abstraction from them; but it can be found here because this is a universal necessarily finding application in every least portion of conduct. This conception is obscurely at work in human life from its lowliest beginnings, shaping and guiding desire and affection, and at work equally in the highest reaches of human genius and heroism. In all action there is effort, for effort is the law of life; but the conception provides a criterion by which the effort may be justified in itself, not merely for what it brings. There need not, however, be conflict, as when conscience is said to make us cowards or duty to fall out with desire. Such internal conflicts, however frequent they may be, spring from avoidable defects, and are therefore pathological. It is the most serious surrender of the true claims of morality to give in to the popular error that morality is involved only where such conflicts exist; but it would be even more fatally foolish to deny the reality of these conflicts and their vital importance in the life of the individual. And if all this is right, the task of the moral philosopher is simply and sufficiently defined as that of defining this conception of action and its applications. He will have to show how out of its collisions with the circumstances of life arise our distinctions of good and bad, of right and wrong, of duty and desire, and all other familiar features of the problem of conduct. Further, if he is to remain true to the name of philosopher, he will have to show also the relation between these moral values and others which the human spirit is no less concerned to maintain.

With the wider issues I am not now concerned. I must be content with indicating in this cursory way that for me too they exist. One thing only remains, by way of conclusion, for me to do—to relate what I have said to the problem stated at the outset and show how, to my mind, it relieves it. We began by recognizing two kinds of value relevant to action; those which a spectator will assert an action itself to possess when he calls it a good or fine action, and those which an agent credits to things round him when he shows an active preference, e.g. for a tidy over an untidy room. I took an example of conflict in which the agent is supposed to modify a course of action which he had already begun and felt inclined to continue, not because of any flaw in the original calculation, but as we say for some moral scruple. This scruple was supposed to be occasioned by an act of imaginative self-judgment in which he regarded himself as from without and saw that his action was not good. But this we felt could not be the normal and characteristic expression of the moral principle. For how much better if he had been directly inclined by his natural benevolence to the right course of action instead of being indirectly forced into it by the fear of self-condemnation! Are we to think, as some moralists have thought, that it is the fear of the pains of self-reproach or the love of the delights of self-approbation that makes men moral? Every unsophisticated mind will be against us here, and will agree rather with Marcus Aurelius in preferring the man who 'has no conception that he has done anything whatever, but may be compared to the vine that bears her grapes and seeks nothing more when once she has done her work and ripened her fruit'. 'A man who has done a good deed', he says, 'should be like a horse that has run its race, a dog that has tracked its game, or a bee that has gathered its honey'.

Now the question of the kinds and modes of self-consciousness is much too large a question to introduce at the tail end of a discussion like this. But I may remind you that those very Stoic philosophers, from whom Marcus Aurelius learned thus to prize unself-consciousness in well-doing, themselves insisted that self-consciousness was of the essence of morality. So that clearly some distinctions are necessary here. In the meantime surely the conception at which we have arrived does throw some light on the matter.

There are these two sets of values, no doubt, but neither of them is ultimate. They are only two manifestations of something more fundamental, of the demand of action that it shall complete its nature and justify itself. The fact of conflict and hesitation does certainly show that this completion is not reached; and the victory of right, however creditable, does certainly imply a possible better state in which right would have had no opponent. So far the earlier interpretation is confirmed. But this better is not something better than morality: it is morality itself. For the judgment of oneself in action which is of the essence of morality is not a judgment of praise and blame, in which a man sees his own acts with the same eyes as those of his friends, and rejoices or despairs accordingly, making all allowances for defective equipment and restricting circumstance; it is something far more persistent and exacting than that, and much less respectful of existing fact. It is the tormenting consciousness of a stricter logic, a higher level of execution, always within reach if the spirit is willing, which leaves no room for rest or contentment, but yet justifies the act so far as it succeeds in pressing its claim. It is not egoism or altruism; it is no thought of self or others, or of the relation between them. But it may take Spinoza's name, the *conatus in suo esse perseverandi*, 'the effort to persevere in one's own being': for he who is committed to living is committed to living as well as he can.

# 4

# *Is There a Moral End?*

I suppose we shall be agreed that positive moral significance belongs to any action in which a man does what he thinks right because he thinks it right. To act thus is to adopt the distinctively moral attitude, just as to create what is beautiful because it is beautiful is to adopt the distinctively aesthetic attitude. The question proposed for this discussion is a question as to the further interpretation of this attitude. In particular: has the man who so acts some end, aim, or purpose in view, and does he accept the act which he adopts and reject its alternatives as consistent and inconsistent respectively with this end? Does the judgment that this act which I now propose to do is the right thing to do allow of such analysis that the act may be seen as a means to an end? Is there a moral good which is furthered in every action which has a positive moral value? To this question I wish to propose a negative answer. If we may term the practical attitude in question the moral attitude and its motive the moral motive, my thesis is that the moral attitude and motive are not purposive.

Man first shows his reasonableness in action by making action purposive, and in purpose means and end necessarily fall apart. For mere impulse there is neither means nor end: there is only a blind fumbling after action of a certain pattern and tendency, as the occasion offers scope for it. By purpose we see the occasion as opportunity, we value it for what we can make of it, and we take care to act so that the results of our action, near and remote, are likely to be such as we shall welcome when they come. The mere impulse to eat will lead us to eat what is bad for us—or if it does not, the credit is Nature's, not ours; but, harnessed to purpose, eating is stimulated and restrained in view of some end, to keep strong and well, to enjoy oneself, to live within one's income. Within the limits set by the end or ends conceived the purposed action is guaranteed, so far as there is no error in the calculation, as good: the action is reasonable and can explain itself.

But on these lines action never becomes wholly reasonable. It is never able fully to explain itself. Both end and means are seen on analysis to contain surds or unexplained remainders. That certain kinds of things or activity interest and amuse us, certain others do not, is a fact not easily altered and indeed not fundamentally alterable; and on such facts all practicable purposes depend for their end. These interests are what Butler called 'particular affections': they mark out certain things as good, and the goodness of the things thus marked out is presupposed in the purposive attitude. 'Self-love', says Butler, 'does not constitute *this* or *that* to be our interest or good; but, our interest or good being constituted by Nature and supposed, self-love only puts us upon obtaining and securing it'. Butler speaks of self-love; but it does not matter, so far as I can see, in what terms the purposive attitude is conceived, whether as directed to self-interest, one's own happiness, or to the greatest happiness of the greatest number, or even as self-realization: in each case this limitation stands, that the end is 'constituted by Nature and supposed' in the purposive activity. So much of the end.

That the means can never rid itself of a certain accidental and contingent character, and remains in external relation to the end which it helps to realize, this is, I suppose, generally conceded, but it is not always grasped how deep-seated this contingency is, and the proper consequences are not always drawn. The difficulty is concealed and slurred over by loose and misleading applications of the terminology of purpose where it does not apply. End and means are allowed to 'coincide', or the moral non-purposive attitude to persons is described as an attitude which treats them as ends-in-themselves. Such attempts to save the face of purpose should at least be postponed until we have seen that face and considered whether it is worth saving.

The discovery of means to a given end is essentially the discovery of a causal nexus. Means are called means so far as they are productive of something else which is called end; and their value lies in their capacity to produce this. One element in the means selected to any end must always be a certain expenditure of effort and energy by the agent; and this effort, being a means, has its value not in itself but for what it produces. Further the best means is that which involves the least expenditure of effort; thus the purposive activity has no value for itself, but implies an ideal in which it is wholly superseded, a state of affairs in which all our ends are realized without activity on our part. The ground of both characteristics is to be found in the severe abstraction of the purposive attitude. It examines a situation solely with a view to its possible contribution to a development regarded as desirable. But the elements which are capable of assisting this development have also a nature of their own, rich in other possibilities, and, even while contributing to the development desired, will also necessarily be assisting other developments which the limitations set by the purpose in hand will conceal from view or dismiss as irrelevant. The agent, similarly, is a man with a human nature, of which this purpose and the effort it exacts from him is only a partial and temporary manifestation; and if his individuality is to be saved, that can only be by some act and attitude which corrects and supplements purpose by a more concrete view of the situation. Purpose alone will never fully justify action to itself.

These very simple considerations suffice, I hope, to show what I mean when I say that any account of action in terms of purpose must be incomplete and defective. If their substantial correctness is conceded, it does not of course follow that there is no moral purpose; only that, if there is, it will provide an explanation of action exhibiting these defects. Probably, then, the best way to proceed will be to take certain admitted characteristics of the moral attitude and see how far these agree or are reconcilable with our diagnosis of the purposive attitude.

First, it is admitted by writers of widely different schools of thought that the claims of morality, as they operate in human life, present on the face of it a very different appearance from the claims of policy or purpose. They come as a recognized obligation to do or not to do, which is often seen to involve the temporary surrender or restriction of a desire in itself innocent, of a perfectly legitimate purpose. All serious moralists have had to recognize this very obvious and familiar contrast. Even the Greeks, in spite of their pre-occupation with purpose, were unable wholly to deny the difference in kind between the moral and the purposive attitude. For Plato the virtue of the philosopher, who has passed beyond all calculation of profit and loss, is the only virtue which deserves the name. In Aristotle's *Ethics* the moral act is an act wholly inspired by love of itself: it is τοῦ καλοῦ ἕνεκα, i.e. directed to its own beauty or nobility; and he makes no attempt whatever to show that this motive is merely an ultimate clarification of the motive operating in less deserving action. On the contrary, he speaks always as if it were a motive peculiar to the good man and different in kind from others. It is not necessary to multiply instances. Butler speaks of the magisterial exertions of conscience; Kant of the categorical, as opposed to the hypothetical, imperative; and John Stuart Mill has to recognize as the most serious objection to the theory of utility, the apparently absolute and imperative character of the claims of justice. In explaining this absolute away as the socially salutary, but theoretically indefensible, conversion of a difference in degree into a difference in kind, he took the course which must I believe in the end be taken by all who believe that morality is purposive. **In** a word: *purpose will not yield 'right' and 'wrong'*.

Secondly, let us consider the judgment of a spectator, or of the agent himself in retrospect, attributing moral value or

73

dis-value to an action which has been done. It will be admitted that this judgment is often uncomfortably sharp and decisive; but as much could be said of judgments recognizing failure in reference to purpose. The point is that hear again there is an apparent difference in kind, which has to be explained away by the champion of purpose. Failure to button a collar, to mend a toy for a child, to secure election to an office—all these are mortifying in their degree. The aims differ in importance; and one failure is more difficult to recover from , both in fact and in temper, than another. But what have these in common with the condemnation of treachery, or the remorse of the traitor? The instances of purpose chosen are all cases in which failure or success declares itself at once; but this is the exception rather than the rule. Often we must wait for years before we know whether our efforts are justified by success. But in moral judgment, many as the obscurities are, even in judging oneself, this complication never enters. Judgment is in no sense or degree conditional upon the actual event. In a word: *purpose will not yield 'good' and 'bad'*.

Thirdly, it is generally admitted that the action upon which moral praise and blame are directed is something to which motive is central. An act done with a bad motive, may, it is supposed, be right (i.e. it may correspond generally in externals with the course of action which a good man in that situation would feel obliged to follow), but it cannot be morally good and deserving of praise. This seems to mean that in praise and blame the action is considered as the external expression of a spiritual state or activity, and that it is this activity as so expressed that is praised or blamed. Now clearly the typical end is a result external to the activity which helps to produce it. Often like victory, peace, prosperity, it comes as a longed for event or an ascent to a new level of life, closing a doubtful struggle on a lower plane. So obvious is this that our professed champion of purpose, the utilitarian, can find no place for motive within the act. 'Motive', in Mill's well-known statement, 'has nothing to do with the morality of the action, though much with the worth of the agent'. A good motive, he means, is one which normally issues in socially profitable action; but, if exceptionally such a motive issues in unprofitable action, we must not be deterred by habitual respect for a valuable motive from recognizing the badness of the act. Apparently, however, our estimate of the agent is not to be affected by our condemnation of the act, which amounts to a confession that this will not be a moral condemnation of the act after all. I have not finished with this point, but I will sum it up in the words; *purpose excludes motive from moral judgment.*

There offers in this connection a rather tempting opening to a return to purpose by means of some notion of self-affirmation or self-realization. Many great names, including Aristotle and Spinoza, and, among moderns, T. H. Green and F. H. Bradley, might be cited as at least partially endorsing a purposive interpretation of morality in this sense. If the end is a state of oneself (it may be argued) then the present state, by which it is to be achieved, must be more than a mere means, since its externality to the end is broken down. The identity of the person through his successive acts destroys the contingency of the means in relation to the end. The means acquire a certain intrinsic value by their intimate relation to the end; while the fact of growth and development of character still justifies a certain emphasis on future results. The self to be realized or affirmed in moral action is not (so Bradley tells us) the actual or particular self; it is a whole. It is not an exclusive self, 'a repellent point or . . . mere individual'; it is a social self. 'The self which is myself, which is mine, is not merely me.' Thus the self which is to be realized both does and does not exist. So far as it does not exist, we are entitled to find purpose, achievement, controlled progress towards an end, in the moral attitude: for an end, as Bradley says, 'is something to be reached, otherwise not an end'. So far as it does exist, the moral attitude may be regarded as conferring absolute value on the actual, and we may say either that the notion of end drops out, since this self is not something to be reached, or that means and end here coincide. On these lines we are offered a reconciliation between purpose and its critics, which is to do justice to the truth contained in each of the opposing views.

I have not space to examine the foundations of this formula of self-realization. Bradley bases it on psychological considerations which to me are far from convincing. I do not think it is true that 'in desire what we want, so far as we want it, is ourselves in some form, or is some state of ourselves; . . . our wanting anything else would be psychologically inexplicable'. Nor, even if that were accepted, would it follow that the moral effort is an attempt to achieve some state of ourselves; for it is not self-evident that all action is the expression of desire. But the insecurity of these foundations is not our present concern. Whatever the arguments may be by which it is justified, the formula of self-realization owes its popularity largely to the fact that it seems to offer an answer to the question, 'Why should I be moral?' (this is the title of Bradley's essay from which I have ben quoting), i.e. that it appears to offer an interpretation of morality in terms of purpose and end. We must remember that it was advanced in fact by these English writers, as an alternative to utilitarianism. It is on this side that it requires examination here.

I fully admit that if we are to state morality in terms of purpose, we must make the end 'ourselves in some form or some state of ourselves', and that self-realization, by offering such an end, escapes some of the worst inadequacies of other purposive interpretations. I would also admit that the doctrine of self-realization is sometimes so stated that none of the objections made above to a purposive interpretation seem to touch it at all. But I should claim that in these latter statements the element of purpose, which is not really essential to the doctrine, has been tacitly suppressed; and that where the interpretation is genuinely purposive, though the formula of self-realization is more adequate to the facts, in the sense that it makes possible a less viciously abstract view of them, it obscures the essence of morality quite as effectually as any other purposive interpretation.

Self-realization is conceived purposively when it is taken to mean the conscious development of the potentialities of the self by action, even if these potentialities are supposed to be such as will eventually be expressed in action. It is the future reference, the emphasis on development, that is crucial; and it is this that in my opinion is irreconcilable with the data of the moral consciousness. I do not of course deny that it is possible, legitimate, and even (within limits) laudable to aim at the development of one's character or at what we often call (following a usage fixed by Aristotle) moral improvement. What I maintain is that whole-hearted attention to this aim will not ensure the rightness of the action in which it is expressed; and that it is so far from being the essence of morality that in certain circumstances it may be condemned as immoral. I think that the formula of self-realization and the writings of those who maintain it lend themselves to the interpretation which I have given, and that in this respect it is a misleading doctrine.

The moral attitude is essentially a concern for the rightness of action. A true instinct exhibits it as interfering with the execution of purpose in stigmatizing as immoral the doctrine that the end justifies the means. The phrase implies that morality requires that all means shall be justified in some other way and by some other standard than their value for this or any end: that however magnificent is the prospect opened out by the proposed course of action, and however incontestable the power of the means chosen to bring this prospect nearer, there is still always another question to be asked: not a question whether in achieving this you will not perhaps diminish your chances of achieving something still more important; but a question of another kind. 'There is a decency required', as Browning said; and this demand of decency is prepared to sacrifice, in the given case, any purpose whatever. If the call of duty were the expression of a purpose, it would have to be a purpose which embraced all purposes from which all others could be shown as derivative, including all creation and even eternity in its scope. We are offered instead our own moral perfection. But what is that to put in the scale against the interests of humanity, the fortunes of countless generations yet unborn? As judges of actions and motives we should rejoice to see a man jeopardizing his own moral development when thereby he seemed to serve the 'greatest happiness of the greatest number'. Thus our moral consciousness asures us: (1) that the end does not justify the means, i.e. that there is no end whatever by which alone the detail of action can be guaranteed as right; (2) that a man's own development or moral perfection is not the highest end to which his action can be directed.

Thus if self-realization is to be retained as descriptive of the moral attitude, it must, first, be deprived of all reference to the future. So far as morality involves the consciousness of doing right, it involves the affirmation and approval of a state of the self; but this state is an actual state and is approved in itself, not as the germ of some future state. Secondly, the state which is approved has no essential self-reference at all. In it the concern for the rightness of action expresses itself in right action, and the action itself has such reference to self and others as the circumstances may dictate. The activity as a whole is no more properly described as self-realization than the activity of painting a picture, or working out a mathematical problem, or any other successful human enterprise. Thus self-realization becomes a purely formal conception which fails to touch the distinctive characteristics of the moral attitude.

So far I have been arguing that morality is not purposive; that the hypothesis of a moral purpose is inadequate to the facts, whether the end proposed to it is outside the self (as 'the greatest happiness of the greatest number') or falls within it (as in the doctrine of self-realization). To complete my statement it is now only necessary for me to consider briefly the question of the precise place of purpose in the concrete act in which the moral value is realized.

Action is always the alteration of a situation, the state of the self being a feature of the situation altered: and, whatever else action is, it must always remain that. In deliberate action the situation is intentionally altered, and, since intention and purpose are inseparable, such action is purposive. If action is to deserve its name, to be fully willed (and evidently much that passes for action is not fully willed), the alterations which it introduces must be intentionally introduced. Thus here again there can be no going back. The concrete moral act must be the alteration of a situation, and that alteration must be intentional: the act must be purposive. This means that the agent must needs accept judgment by results. Failure is failure; and its bitterness is not diminished, rather increased, by the conviction that the energy spent fruitlessly in it had another justification. The adequacy of the means adopted in action to the end proposed—and not merely to the end actually in view at the time, but to that in relation to other ends and purposes adopted by the agent; and in relation, further, to the communities of which he is a member and their life and activity—the accurate diagnosis and adjustment of this far-reaching causal nexus is the internal logic of the act, the test by which the agent himself in the moment of action implicitly claims that it shall be judged. If it fails by this test, it fails; but the fault, if fault there be, is a fault of knowledge, of judgment, of imagination, of breadth of vision; never a moral fault. The act is not shown to have been wrong. Complications arise in fact owing to the limitations of knowledge, the different kinds and sources of ignorance, unforeseen contingencies, and so on; but here these may be ignored, and we may say simply that this is the field of purpose and in it action is discriminated by achievement and non-achievement, failure and success.

Morality is to be regarded as supervening upon purpose in the sense that in the moral attitude everything that belongs to purpose is before the mind and none of it is denied. Moral considerations do not arise upon further exploration of the causal nexus, or by the introduction of some wider and deeper purpose, or by the transference of the purposive problem from a purely individual to a social plane. Purpose must complete its own work, which includes all this; but when its work is completed, the problem of conduct is not yet solved. The moral consciousness supervenes with a further demand, which creates the specifically moral aspect of the problem. Until this demand is satisfied no project of action may be passed for execution. The demand is, in short, that the activity of securing a certain many-sided result by a course of action at every point manifold in its implications shall be seen to be in all its stages a fit expression of the human will. The enquiry dictated by this demand differs from enquiries undertaken in the interest of purpose in three main points. First, the action is regarded not as a contribution to the world's welfare, but as a case of spiritual activity or self-expression. Secondly, the transitive character of the process, with the inevitable emphasis on the issue, thus drops into the background: the activity has to justify itself as a whole and in every moment. Thirdly, the values recognized are intrinsic and absolute, not relative and conditional like those of purpose. A project of action which survives this enquiry passes into action which can claim to be fully justified and to be morally justified, and to have a value in itself apart from its results.

The concrete moral act, then, is purposive. If it served no purpose, it would be pointless, and what is pointless cannot be right. But it is a familiar fact that morality often interferes with the execution of our purposes; and it seems that it is just in such conflicts that the most unquestionable moral values are revealed. Surely in such cases at least (it may be urged) morality must supply some purpose of its own, if we are not to be left with a void, with an act which is no act because it is pointless. On this I have two remarks to make. (1) Man has many purposes and interests, and no attempt to reduce them to one has ever been successful. A line of action which obstructs one purpose will assist another. And, in fact, it is impossible to find a moral command or prohibition which has no support from expediency, though in many cases proof may be unattainable that the line of action enjoined is the most expedient open to the agent. Thus the action need not be pointless because it runs counter in its effect to the ruling purpose.

(2) What morality approves or rejects, in part or as a whole, is a concrete purposing, not in general or in respect merely of its direction, but as worked out in its full detail and in every detail of it. To this its response is immediate and intuitive. The moral judgment, like the aesthetic judgment, does not argue and cannot be argued. All that can be done, in case of dispute, is to call attention to details in the object for which approval or disapproval is claimed, which may have escaped attention or received less than their proper weight. Hence the main part of the discussion of a disputed moral judgment will be conducted in terms of means and end, and will concern what are called the consequences of the act. The rest will be a reassertion of the variance of the intuitive judgment at each point. It is this that gives rise to the illusion that the whole dispute can be reduced to a question of means and end. But though the judgment is immediate and intuitive and cannot be argued, yet in morality, as in art, reflective analysis can detect principles at work in it. To extract these principles and define them is the main task of the branch of philosophy which has morality for its subject. The whole history of ethics suggests that any sound analysis of moral judgments will find at work in them, not merely a conception of the dignity of human nature, of its proper organization and deportment, as something to be maintained by the individual agent in all his actions, but also of the relation of man to man in society and in a spiritual kingdom, perhaps, to which religion alone gives entry. But when the philosophical analysis has been completed and the metaphysical foundations of the moral judgment have been finally laid bare, we shall have to recognize that these principles were all along operative in shaping human desires and the purposes in which they are co-ordinated, and that the limitations imposed on desire by purpose and on purpose by morality were therefore no external and arbitrary interferences but corrections demanded by the inner logic of the impulse or purpose itself.

# 5

## *The Golden Mean*

A famous phrase with a long history, such as that which stands at the head of this page, is apt to carry a certain savour or quality of its own, largely independent of its actual historical associations. To my ear at least, 'The Golden Mean' has quite pleasant, but rather trivial quality, recalling by its immediate suggestions no ardour of speculation, no energy of theoretical or other enterprise, but rather the worldly wisdom of a cultured and contented circle, secure in the possession of the best that the life of its time had to offer. We think at once of the Augustan age of ancient Rome, or of its parallel (as we often regard it) in our own eighteenth century. It is perhaps fitting then to introduce what I have to say by two quotations from this period of English literature, which fall in with what I take to be the immediate suggestions of the phrase.

The first belongs to the middle of the eighteenth century. It is from a poem by the successful Irish adventurer, George Bubb Dodington, Lord Melcombe, a 'person of importance in his day', as Browning reminds us. The poem is to be found in the *Oxford Book of English Verse* under the title 'Shorten Sail'.

> Love thy country, wish it well,
> Not with too intense a care;
> Tis enough that when it fell
> Thou its ruin didst not share.

82

So the poem begins. It proceeds to recommend indifference to envy and flattery, and generally virtue, as the clue to the 'dangerous maze' of life.

> Void of strong desire and fear,
>     Life's wide ocean trust no more;
> Strive thy little bark to steer
>     With the tide, but near the shore.

On these terms, the poet tells us, our 'shortened sail' will bring us by an easy passage to the port of Peace—

> Easy shall thy passage be,
>     Cheerful thy allotted stay,
> Short the account twixt God and thee,
>     Hope shall meet thee on thy way.

My second quotation is earlier in date. It falls in fact outside the eighteenth century altogether. It is taken from the conclusion of Halifax's brilliant political essay, *The Character of a Trimmer*, published in 1688.

> Our Trimmer, therefore (writes Halifax), inspired by this divine virtue, thinks fit to conclude with these assertions—That our Climate is a Trimmer, between that part of the world where men are roasted and the other where they are frozen; That our Church is a Trimmer, between a frenzy of Platonic visions and the lethargic ignorance of Popish dreams; That our laws are Trimmers, between the excess of unbounded power and the extravagance of liberty not enough restrained: That true virtue hath ever been thought a Trimmer, and to have its dwelling in the middle between the two extremes; That even God Almighty is divided between his two great attributes, his mercy and his justice. In such company our Trimmer is not ashamed of his name; and willingly leaveth to the bold champions of either extreme the honour of contending with no less adversaries than Nature, Religion, Liberty, Prudence, Humanity, and Common Sense.

These, with innumerable other similar utterances, derive of course ultimately from the Aristotelian doctrine of the Mean. Bubb Dodington's unheroic counsel of Safety

First, and Halifax's witty plea for compromise as the ultimate political principle—both alike, so far as they appeal to authority, would appeal to the authority of Aristotle, to the wise empiricist who revolted against the high-flying fancies of his master, Plato. They would be speaking in a familiar tradition, as to the sources of which they did not trouble themselves. I do not suppose that either of them was much of a Greek scholar. Without going to Aristotle himself, they might have found in Milton's *Areopagitica* a much truer version of the celebrated doctrine. In a leading passage of his eloquent plea for unlicensed printing, Milton had argued that virtue cannot be created by removing occasion for vice, since it consists in right choice by one who is free to choose between good and evil. 'Wherefore', he asks, 'did he [God] create passions within us, pleasures round about us, but that these rightly tempered are the very ingredients of virtue? . . . Suppose we could expel sin by this means; look how much we thus expel of sin, so much we expel of virtue: for the matter of them both is the same; remove that, and ye remove them both alike'. There is nothing, however, here to tell the uninstructed reader that the doctrine is that of Aristotle, or to connect it with the mean. And, in the whole history of English literature who is there fit to stand beside Milton as a scholar? On this point, further, his voice sounds alone in all the centuries. Our first two quotations may seriously misrepresent the sense and spirit of the original doctrine, but they must be allowed to stand as typical of the repute in which it stood.

II

But it is with the doctrine itself, not the popular travesty of it, that I am now concerned. I want to state it in what I take to be its fundamentals and consider briefly its value as a contribution to the theory of conduct. I ought, however, first to say that it is not distinctively Aristotelian, even in its ethical form. It is part of a general metaphysical doctrine of universal application, which did not originate with Aristotle or even with Plato, but is a characteristic feature of the main current of the Greek philosophical tradition. In expounding his ethical doctrine Aristotle seems to claim that he is only developing notions which are commonplaces of the schools. It is pretty certain from a number of passages in the Platonic dialogues that a similar ethical doctrine was current in the school of Plato. And the parallels in other quarters are sufficient to justify the assertion that in its essence the doctrine received something like general acceptance and may be taken as forming a part of the typical Greek view of life.

I will begin with two illustrative analogies which Aristotle himself uses—first, that of a work of art, and secondly, that of bodily health.

Of a work of art, he says, it is commonly observed that nothing can be added or taken away. It is, or strives to be, complete; and this completeness depends on the maintenance of due proportion between the parts or factors which together compose it. Each component must be right in quantity if the result which we call beauty is to be achieved. Strengthen or weaken the colour, increase or diminish the size of this or that; and the total effect is lost or damaged. Thus art is seen to maintain its footing precariously on a razor's edge between too much and too little: by innumerable delicate quantitative adjustments it reaches its goal. Beauty is no doubt a quality, not a quantity; but the quality is reached and realized through quantity.

A similar result emerges from an analysis of bodily health, and its maintenance. In the human body opposites are always at war, dry with moist, warm with cold, and health depends on the maintenance of the balance of power, on due mixture or temperament. Within certain narrow limits the balance may change, the proportions alter, as summer and winter succeed one another in the sequence of the seasons; but beyond these limits disease begins. Heat must not be allowed to establish a tyranny over a part of the body, as when one has an inflamed finger, or over the whole organism, as when a man is in a fever. Such encroachments of contrary on contrary are eventually destructive of the organism. Now health is not just this balance of opposites. It must be defined positively as the discharge of certain functions; and such discharge of function cannot be expressed in quantitative ratios. But this performance of function is continuously conditioned by the maintenance of certain quantitative ratios in the material substratum concerned.

Two striking sayings of an earlier generation are brought together in these observations. Heracleitus had found the formula of substance in the 'adjustment of opposed tensions, as of the bow and the lyre'. And the famous sculptor Polycleitus, in the only surviving sentence of his *Canon*, is reported to have said: 'that which is well comes into being little by little by means of many numbers'. In terms of Aristotle's favourite phraseology of matter and form, the generalization which these examples are meant to suggest is this: that, in order to impose form on matter, all that is needed is to adjust quantitatively the material ingredients: from such adjustment form emerges.

It is perhaps worth noting here, before we go on to the ethical application, that there is another aspect of human life in which Aristotle seems to find this principle at work. The analysis of sensation in his psychology is carried out by means of terms similar to those used in the analysis of virtue. Sensation also is called a mean: sensitive activity requires a balance of opposites in the organ, in the medium and in the stimulus: its enemies also are thus excess and defect, which beyond a certain point preclude the sensitive activity and may eventually impair or destroy the sense organ. The detail of the argument is somewhat obscure, and Aristotle gives no indication in either treatise that he is conscious of an identity of principle in his treatment of the two problems. But the identity of principle is there, and Aristotle's unconsciousness of it (if he was unconscious of it) is only further evidence of how deep-rooted this general conception was in his thought.

To secure the outline of the ethical doctrine, all we need to do is to specify the matter and the form involved; and since the form gives the end, there will remain only the fourth of Aristotle's causes, the stimulus or efficient cause. We shall have to ask then further, what guides or controls as from without, the process of development, the process, as we might say, of information.

The form to be realized is of course virtue, or, more precisely, virtuous character. For virtuous conduct requires according to Aristotle a right state of the intelligence as well as of the character, and it is the development of character that is to be described as a mean, not that of the intelligence. Now character lives in its expression, which is action. Thus the material is the material of action, which is twofold, external and internal. We see an act as an external movement, and we find efficient action where the visible movements are duly co-ordinated in view of some foreseen issue. But we have reason to know also that this external control is preconditioned by an internal discipline which reduces to order the wayward impulses of man's emotional or passionate nature. Thus it is man's desires and emotions which constitute primarily the matter in which virtue of character is to be realized. As long as we remember that the external expression is always involved, we may put it on one side and think of this excellence of character as manifested in desire and emotion.

Simplifying the question thus, we are asked by Aristotle's principle to accept this ruling: that these desires and emotions are neither good nor bad, but are material, in itself neutral, out of which, by certain different arrangements and adjustments to environment, what we call goodness and badness is made: that the positive achievement which we call goodness comes, not by elimination of certain elements as bad, or by the introduction of some new factor which is the soul of goodness, but simply by the right arrangement and adjustment of these materials. There is, as Aristotle amply recognizes, a further factor to be reckoned with here, the tenacity of the organism which makes such things as skill and habit possible. To this factor we owe it that we have some security for the maintenance and repetition of such achievements as good action or the healthy functioning of the human body. But, looked at in its momentary character, we see virtue, like health and artistic beauty, as a precarious achievement dangerously poised on a number of fine adjustments and liable at any moment to lose that poise and fall into its opposite. For the ingredients of good and of bad are precisely the same.

Now the antithesis of matter and form, as conceived by Aristotle, is not absolute. There is not something which is eternally and essentially material. What we refer to in a given context as matter is a substance actually so organized as to occupy a certain defined position in the scale of being, but capable also of being raised by further organization to a higher level. When the higher level is reached, those to whom the whole scale of being is open will recognize a new creation. What was a piece of marble has become the figure of a god. But it is none the less still a piece of marble; and in terms of the lower or material level the earlier and later states are only quantitatively differentiated. Every feature of the finished product can be exhaustively expressed in such terms. But though the alterations made by the sculptor's chisel are in a sense completely accounted for from the material side, they cannot be understood without recourse to the higher level. Until we bring to our aid specifically artistic conceptions, the shape given to the marble by the sculptor remains obscure and accidental, just one among infinite other possible dispositions of the material. From the higher level the lower point of view is not cancelled, but it is transcended. We see that the elements in the lower organization have been induced, without prejudice to that organization, to redispose themselves so as to become the vehicle of a higher order and organization.

We may recall here Abt Vogler's expression of wonder at the miracle of harmony:

> And I know not if, save in this, such gift be allowed to man
> That out of three sounds he frame, not a fourth sound, but a star.

But if Aristotle is right, the case of music is in no way

exceptional. It is merely one among innumerable other examples of a universal law of natural development. In every natural process latent potentialities are evoked, and the method of this evocation is always in principle the same—the quantitative adjustment of actualities by which actualities of a higher order are generated. Quantity is the appointed mediator between matter and form. Plato had already said this in his myth of the creation. 'Before that time', he wrote, 'all things were without ratio or measure. But when the creator set himself to order the whole, he first differentiated this confusion by means of shapes and numbers' (*Timaeus* 53 a, b).

### III

The doctrine which I have outlined seems, on the face of it, to have much to recommend it, both in its more general aspect and in its special application to the field of ethics. In ethics it seems to hold out the promise of fairly meeting two demands which I think we are most of us nowadays inclined and entitled to make of an ethical theory; that it shall exhibit virtue or goodness as a positive achievement, and not as a mere negation, and that it shall offer an escape from the dualism of the moral and the natural which unsystematic reflection on the problem of conduct is apt to fall into, not without support from ethical writers. This theory would have us believe that in these ethical developments man is not deserting or defying Nature, but building naturally on the natural. The good man is not required to forego the satisfaction of any native instinct or impulse: he is merely to discriminate and watch occasions. Moderation is no doubt enjoined; but this is not a uniform mean intensity of emotion and desire. The appropriate degree of intensity will vary in general within wide limits, but in the particular case will be determined more narrowly, with reference to the situation, in the interest of a total effect. On these terms, it seems, we need not fear to meet either the ascetic or the sensualist: to both we shall have our answer. The doctrine gives us also a point of view which should enable us to go much of the way

---

with the modern psychologist, who states the problems of character in terms of repressions and sublimations of impulse.

As a general theory also the doctrine seems to have a curious affinity, in spite of a fundamental difference in the point of view, with modern theories of Nature. It is not surprising that an evolutionary biologist like Darwin found Aristotle far the most congenial of the ancient writers on his subject. The modern scientific metaphysics of emergent evolution must certainly find a serious obstacle in Aristotle's fundamental disbelief in the possibility that natural process can ever, in the world considered as a whole, bring any genuine novelty to birth. But the principle we are considering is to some extent detachable from this general presupposition, and may claim from these enquirers also at least a respectful interest. We have indeed a recent example of a comprehensive metaphysical scheme, based fundamentally on the natural sciences, which seems to appropriate the Aristotelian principle, thus detached, as a general formula of evolution. General Smuts's book *Holism and Evolution* may be described without serious inaccuracy as a reassertion of the Aristotelian point of view, corrected by the recognition of time and process as ultimate in reality.

It will advance our argument, and lead us eventually back to conduct, if we consider one point in General Smuts's Aristotelianism in some little detail. There is a passage in which, apparently at some friend's request, he states shortly his attitude to Prof. Lloyd Morgan's conception of emergent evolution. He explains that in spite of much agreement there is an essential diversity of theme and emphasis in their thought.

> To him, [he says (p. 321, note)], emergence of the new in the evolution of the universe is the essential fact; to me there is something more fundamental—the character of wholeness, the tendency to wholes, ever more intensive and effective wholes, which is basic to the universe, and of which emergence or creativeness is but one feature, however important it is in other respects. Hence he lays all the emphasis on the feature of emer-

gence, while I stress wholes or Holism as the real factor, from which emergence and all the rest follow.

The issue here is the same as that which divided Plato and Aristotle from certain thinkers of their own day. You will remember how in Plato's *Phaedo* Socrates is represented as complaining of the stupidity of those who think that his presence in the prison, sitting quietly in conversation with his friends, waiting for the poison which will end his life, can be explained completely in terms of the tension and relaxation of the muscles and sinews of the body. For the full statement of the matter, he suggested, another order of causation must be brought in, which refers to purpose and contemplated good. Similarly General Smuts is dissatisfied with a view of evolution which sees a novelty as generated merely by the behaviour of certain pre-existent things, which uses the term emergence to suggest at once that it is and that it is not accounted for by their behaviour. He asks leave to introduce into the process, as an active factor, *the whole* which in the process is maintained and advanced. This is essentially a demand that causation of the normal type, in which the parts determine the whole, shall be supplemented by a causation of another order, in which the whole determines the parts; it is in short a demand that the material shall be supplemented by the formal cause; and this formal cause, he adds, is to be taken as the supreme cause, 'the real factor, from which emergence and all the rest follow'. What he is protesting against is essentially materialism, i.e. the view that the lower determines the higher, and the ground of his protest is in the end the same as that of Plato and Aristotle, that such a view leaves the world-process to the guidance of chance.

I said some time ago that there were three questions that had to be answered in order to apply the Aristotelian principle to conduct. We were to specify the form, the matter, and the actuating principle of the process in which the appropriate matter comes to receive its form. To the first two of these questions I have given some answer; but the third has not yet been considered. Our reference to General Smuts and to his conception of a whole which is an active factor in process brings us back to it. It is clearly Aristotle's view that in a complex which is raised to a higher power by quantitative manipulation the ingredients are not self-regulating. The desires and emotions do not just dispose themselves in the pattern which is virtue. What then is it that presides over their evolutions?

It might be supposed that Aristotle would find the actuating principle in intelligence. It is intelligence, undoubtedly, that enables the architect to devise the architectural form which he embodies in the wood and stone of a building. It is intelligence equally that enables the physician to devise a means for restoring the order of the human body, bringing health out of sickness. But the architect and the physician are separated from that on which they work. To conceive the intelligence of the man who grows in virtue as actuating that growth would be to assert a similar separation between his intelligence and his emotional nature, to give intelligence a detachment and a freedom which is irreconcilable with any sound psychology. Hence, though Aristotle will say that the right state of the practical intelligence necessarily presupposes the presence of every virtue, he makes it sufficiently clear that this unerring judgment of value is only to be secured as the fruit of sound discipline in emotion and action. Consequently the objection which he thinks himself most likely to meet is that his theory of virtue reduces the intelligence to impotence; for the justice and courage and temperance which it rightly values must already be possessed before it can rightly value them. The guiding principle then of the development must be sought elsewhere.

We have here surely a genuine difficulty, which General Smuts's formula of Holism equally has to face. How can that which is to be born, which therefore does not yet exist, control the process which brings it to birth? Of course any complex at any moment in its development may be regarded as some sort of a whole; and it may be important to recognize in the behaviour of any living thing a factor describable as the reaction of the whole in this sense on the components. But if the whole is no more than this, it can only be a conservative influence: it cannot be a principle reaching out beyond the actual to new creations. Holism in this sense may point to a real factor, but not to a factor from which emergence follows. If emergence is to follow, the whole which operates as an active factor in the process must be the whole which the process is generating; and such a whole as operative the argument will not grant us.

From this difficulty, which appears and reappears in the most varied forms, Aristotle seeks to extricate himself in a variety of ways. His stock phrase 'man begets man' puts the grown man firmly before the baby in time, as actuating the process by which another fully equipped creature of the same kind comes gradually into existence. His assertion that there is a divine principle in all things suggests, rather vaguely, an unlimited capacity in each thing to transcend its actual limits. A similar suggestion is conveyed by his free use of terms of desire or appetition at every level of being, as though these terms implied a direction towards an absolute good. The famous chapter in the *Metaphysics* which exhibits God as the unmoved mover, who draws the love of all things to his changeless perfection and so accounts for all the movements of the world, is only the final substantiation of these tendencies. Here at last is an actual absolute perfection, capable of accounting for any approximation to itself in the detail of the system which it completes.

On the human level and in the special case of the moral problem Aristotle certainly finds in man a general desire or wish for good unqualified, which he seems to relate to appetites like hunger and thirst much as he relates thought to sensation. One might expect therefore that moral development would be mainly actuated, so far as it is actuated from without, by persuasion or instruction from those who know and are therefore qualified to teach what is really good, so that through a pupil's intelligence a re-orientation of his whole life may be effected. For he will surely seek the good which he desires, once he is shown what it is and convinced that there are ways of getting it. But in fact Aristotle is far from any such view. He does mention casually that instruction has some part to play in moral development, but he gives no special emphasis or detail to his assertion. Clearly he had no temptation to the overdrawn confidence of men like Godwin in the omnipotence of truth and the all-sufficiency of persuasion. It is on education that he like them relies; but his education is not an affair of teaching and preaching which shall mould men's lives through their opinions, such as the French Revolution looked for: it is a much wider conception. The forces of a fully organized and equipped social life continuously operating on the citizen from the very moment of his birth through every channel by which such forces can operate—these are Aristotle's educators. So far as he does not rely on some hidden internal spring of virtue or on some half-mystical conception of Nature as predetermining the issue of the processes in which she consists, the formative influence on which he relies is that of the organized city-state. The whole structure of his *Ethics* and *Politics* implies this.

## IV

We have now spent a considerable time wandering about the territory in which the theory of the Mean is at home, and we must prepare to return to our own country with some report of our wanderings. It is the problem of conduct and the conception of the moral good with which we are specially concerned. It is on this side that we are particularly invited to compare the two countries. But as soon as we try to do this, we find comparison difficult. While we remain within the circle of Greek ideas, the doctrine seems interesting and enlightening and leaves little opening to damaging criticism. But we turn to our modern authors, and the whole matter wears a fundamentally different aspect. We are confronted at once with plain and absolute distinctions between right and wrong, with a magisterial conscience which anticipates the divine sentence on the evildoer, with the stern law-giver duty. In place of an order gradually achieved through discipline and enjoying its own perfection, we are asked to accept the intimidating thunders of the categorical imperative. Even our utilitarians, who are frankly at war with this side of our tradition, demand that the development of the self shall be strictly subordinated to the service of humanity. What is the meaning of this difference?

If we look at the records we possess of the conduct of the ancient Greeks and consider the contemporary judgments upon it that have been preserved, we do not find that their estimates differed at all widely from ours. There may be differences of emphasis, but on the whole they admired the same things that we admire and in much the same degree. For them, as for us, it was an act of signal heroism when a man voluntarily gave his life for his friend or for his country or for a principle. Asceticism—the call to the extirpation of the passions—is no modern invention. It was an alternative almost as present to Aristotle as to ourselves. There is of course the great difference between the two ages that the one has the Christian ideal before it and the other had not; and to this, if you like, you may credit the whole difference in the point of view. But if I am right in saying that the actions praised and blamed by the Greeks were in the main the same as those we praise and blame today, there still remains a question worth asking about the Greeks. Why did they—or more particularly, why did Aristotle—fail to see the supreme significance of such actions of self-sacrifice and self-denial as those we have mentioned, or try to reduce them by some spurious arithmetic to cases of self-seeking? Was there perhaps some element in the general attitude which forced these into the background? Why has duty so small a place in Aristotle's thought that there is not even a word for it?

The answer seems to me to be in brief this. What the theory we have been considering has defined, and on the whole defined rightly, is the terms on which that power of free self-determination, which we call will, can be attained and maintained. It is a victory over internal disorder. What the theory has failed to define is the conditions of the exercise of that freedom when it has been attained. The answer to this second and more important question is what we miss both in their Ethics and in their Politics; and its absence is the reason for the absence of any account of either duties or rights.

The general principle of Aristotle's thought is sometimes called an immanent teleology. That is, he thinks of the movements of all things as directed to an end, but to an end within themselves; he thinks of all natural movement as self-realization. In following his thought on the ethical plane we have moved throughout, in obedience to his directions, within the circle of the self, with its development and perfection for our ultimate term. We have seen how within that circle order requires the acceptance of due limits by each component of the whole. We have watched the whole, which is the self, imposing limits on its subordinates and components. But we have not placed the self in any wider context in which similarly the demand of order and system would require its subordination. It is only when from such a wider point of view we see individual wills in co-operation that duty and self-sacrifice come into view. On its more negative side duty appears as a restraint upon the individual and a limitation of his freedom of choice. But this negative is only the shadow cast by a positive. As a member of a community which he with other individuals forms—a family, a club, a city or a nation—he has to accept principles of conduct which cannot be deduced from a study of his nature alone, but only from the study of the new combination into which he enters. We have failed to reach this point because Aristotle failed to reach it. His immanent teleogy issues in an ethics which stops short at the frontiers of morality.

This summary estimate of the elements of truth and untruth in the doctrine we have been considering may seem to have one very paradoxical feature. Classical Greek theory tended to join ethics and politics; we separate them. Class-

ical Greek theory aggrandized the state as the custodian of
morality: we refuse to trust it so far. The Greek, we have
been taught to think, was before all things a citizen. If that
is so, it may be said, there must be something wrong with
an analysis which traces the difference between their ethical
view and ours to lack of recognition on their part of the
social foundations of the moral problem. A full discussion
of this objection would require a detailed comparison of
ancient and modern theories of government, which is here
out of the question. Such a comparison would soon show
how treacherous some of our familiar labels are. We
moderns are individualists perhaps in a sense in which they
were not; but they are individualists, too, even more
obstinately and profoundly, in their own way. Modern
individualism has given a negative colour to theories of
government, prescribing limits to its action and responsibility, where the Greeks seem to make no reserve. 'The City',
says Aristotle, 'must mould to its purpose the bodies of new
born babies'. The modern reader shudders on meeting these
words. But the modern theory ever since its sensational
beginnings in America and France, where it took its stand
confidently on the individualism of natural rights, has
always contained, in virtue of its fundamental principle of
popular sovereignty, the belief that political organization
corresponds to some positive element in the will of the
citizen: the citizen is agent rather than patient. We have
shown already that Aristotle's moral theory requires the
State as educator, i.e. as a force operating on the citizen.
But Aristotle is distrustful of democracy, and, if his arguments in partial endorsement of the democratic principle
are examined, they will be found to contain no word suggesting that the conception of the active citizen, cardinal to
modern democratic ideas, had any intrinsic attraction for
him. His individualism, which is perhaps characteristically
Greek, is the fundamental assumption that the activities of
any living thing necessarily return upon itself, that self-
realization is the last word; and this entails a corresponding
negativity in his conception of the State. As the modern

individualism may fail to moralize politics, so the ancient individualism may fail to socialize ethics.

I conclude then that the apparent paradox disappears on closer examination, and that the account given may stand, at least for the present. The conception of virtue as a mean is not a counsel of caution or compromise, as Bubb Dodington and Halifax suggest. It is perfectly compatible with noble and heroic action. But, since it affords no explanation of those acts which are most admired or of the degree of admiration which they attract, it must be regarded as, ethically, of minor significance. The failure of modern moralists to take account of it has, I am afraid, after all some justification.

# 6

# *The Need for a Social Philosophy*

I

In Boswell's *Life of Johnson* the following entry may be found under the year 1755: 'In July this year he had formed some scheme of mental improvement, the particular purpose of which does not appear. But we find in his "Prayers and Meditations", page 25, a prayer entitled "On the Study of Philosophy, as an instrument of living", and after it follows a note, "This study was not pursued", Johnson at the time was forty-six years old. What crisis evoked this pathetic and abortive appeal to philosophy for guidance, Boswell clearly did not know. He makes no comment on the final note in which the hope of assistance from this source is finally dismissed. It is as though the Master had proved his strength once more by overcoming yet another temptation. I sometimes wonder whether this entry in Boswell is not typical of a very general attitude to philosophy, characteristic of most men at most times, and of nearly all societies. For the most part, it is something with which they need not concern themselves and can safely leave alone, which raises unnecessary questions, interesting, perhaps, to intellectual busybodies, but better ignored by practical men, questions probably not capable of final solution and in any case of little moment for the guidance of life. At times, however, things go wrong, and a suspicion stirs in them that in these remote unsolved problems the secret of their perplexities and the solution of them may perhaps be found.

99

Then they may for a time take up 'the study of philosophy, as an instrument of living'. But for most of these after a longer or shorter time a new equilibrium is reached, and the study of philosophy is 'not pursued'.

If this is at all true of the single individual, it is natural that it should be more true of man in the mass and of the societies which men form. One would expect to find that periods of great stability and security would be periods in which the public interest in philosophical speculation was at its minimum; that some deep and far-reaching disturbance of the social equilibrium on one of its many sides would be necessary before the philosopher could claim general attention for his doctrine or find ready assent to his own estimate of the importance of the questions with which he deals. I think there is pretty good historical evidence that this is in fact the case. The chief period in which the English people was deeply interested in political speculation was the period of the Civil Wars and the Commonwealth, when English political institutions were in the melting-pot, and the astonishing outburst of ethical speculation which characterized the first half of the eighteenth century in this country was preceded by a powerful movement of religious scepticism which loosened the hold of religious sanctions on the educated mind of the time. The ferment which accompanied the events of the French Revolution at the end of the eighteenth century in nearly every country in Europe is another example, but in its later stages that disturbance cut too deep, and philosophy itself was thought to have been discredited by its excesses. Hazlitt, who had himself, as he put it, seen the sun of liberty turn in France to blood, described the Revolution as 'the only match that ever took place between philosophy and experience'; and Macaulay wrote of the reaction that followed: 'Freedom was regarded as a great delusion. Men were willing to submit to the government of hereditary princes, of fortunate soldiers, of nobles, of priests: to any government but that of philosophers and philanthropists'. But there is no need to multiply instances. The point is simple and probably obvious; some profound disturbance of the social and intellectual climate is required to bring philosophy into general attention; at other times it remains in the background, respected perhaps, but ignored by those who manage the affairs of men.

These trite reflections have a certain actuality. For we are at the moment living through a period of profound disorder and disturbance; and if there is any truth in what has been said, these disturbances should have produced or be producing an increased demand for the services of the philosopher in the regions affected by the disturbance, if not an unusual outburst of philosophical speculation in matters relevant to it.

It is, in fact, difficult to point to any considerable portion of the field of thought and conduct which is wholly untouched by the radical scepticism and instability characteristic of the time through which we are passing. Everywhere is fluidity, insecurity, lack of final authority and of untroubled certainty. Perhaps one is inclined in retrospect to exaggerate the complacency and stability of the late nineteenth century. But though there were problems, then, and though pessimistic observers of politics, like Leonard Hobhouse, saw the presage of disaster to democracy in the hectic imperialism of the Boer War, and acute interpreters of scientific thought, like James Ward, saw signs of growing weakness in the imposing façade of scientific orthodoxy, yet they were far from carrying everyone with them; and even they must have been surprised before they died at the scope of the revolutions which they saw in progress round them. In the nineteenth century natural science made spectacular advances in every part of its field. Problem after problem was successfully formulated and solved. Methods were devised and perfected by which, as it seemed, this process could be continued indefinitely. The whole field was divided up; for each part of it appropriate methods and principles were found. All that was needed further was a sufficient number of industrious and intelligent workers, who, working each in his own little plot, in co-operation would gradually uncover the last mysteries of nature.

Whether there were, as philosophers said, or were not, as many scientists were inclined to think, further important questions about the world, which such methods as these were impotent to answer, did not really matter. In either case the scientist could go on with his work safely, without troubling his head with them. Metaphysics could be left to metaphysicians.

There can be no doubt that during this present century the confidence of the scientists in their ability to exclude ultimate metaphysical questions and solve the problem of nature by the cumulative effect of piecemeal advances has seriously weakened. They have found themselves forced more and more to question their fundamental assumptions, and thus to enter ground which had been previously reckoned metaphysical. Not unnaturally the philosopher has been tempted to intervene in these discussions, and sometimes, advancing with more zeal than discretion, he has run the risk of appearing to claim the position of legislator for the sciences. There has in fact developed a kind of No Man's Land where scientific philosophers and philosophic scientists engage in controversy as to the propriety of which neither science nor philosophy is assured. The signal example of this tendency is, of course, mathematical physics; but it is not the sole example. There is also the field of biology, in which the old mechanism is questioned by working scientists as well as by philosophers.

More relevant to my present subject is the field of conduct, and here the situation is essentially the same. Our time is plainly characterized by widespread doubt concerning the principles of action, to which the late nineteenth century offers no parallel. In those days the philosopher felt in a sense no great responsibility in this field. His task was merely that of providing a theoretical basis for practical principles securely established and generally recognized. These formed the secure starting-point and the predetermined goal of his speculations; his differences with his brother philosophers were differences of interpretation. He might accept the Utilitarianism of the Benthamite or the

Law of Duty as preached by the followers of Kant, and feel that practically the choice was of little moment. Thus, here, as in science, the philosophical question was isolated and fenced off, after a fashion made possible by the existence in the field of a massive series of immediate certainties, which rightly or wrongly were taken as beyond question. Today these immediate practical certainties seem no longer to exist; the principles of action are themselves questioned and found to need proof. The philosopher therefore does not know where to begin. He is asked to face the novel task of creating his own point of departure. This means that mere interpretation is no longer sufficient; he is called to perform a work of construction. It means, to put it otherwise, that while formerly his work had merely theoretical significance, it now has, or is expected to have, practical importance. He is asked not merely to speculate, but also to preach and edify. Thus once more, as in ancient Greece, the question 'what must I do to be saved?' is addressed to the philosopher; he is expected to commend to his followers a way of life. The task which the advent of the Christian religion seemed to have relieved him of for ever, comes back upon his hands.

Equally in politics and in sociology generally, not excluding economics, the foundations are shaken and the old certainties have become matters of dispute. There is little trace today of any parallel to the splendid confidence with which, before the first Reform Bill, James Mill constructed a deductive science of politics from a few propositions of psychology. All theoretical deductions are paralysed by a general doubt which reaches to their fundamental principles. In politics the geometrical method (to give it John Mill's description) was surrendered long ago; but it was reserved for our own time to disqualify the theoretical economist as well. He is now shown to have been making sociological assumptions to which he had no right, and to have lost his limited application in a changing world. And this general distrust of deduction is not balanced by any compensating confidence in the promise or performance of the inductive method. Plans for positive sciences of politics and society were frequent enough in the nineteenth century; but today little is heard of them. No such sciences exist or seem likely to come into existence. The secure basis for political action, which so many seek, seems very unlikely to be found by any extension of the methods of the natural sciences. Meanwhile the world clamours for guidance in its pressing perplexities. Never has the theorist been so much in demand, and never has he been so uncertain of his own inspiration.

To a great extent, of course, the social and political confusion is simply the same phenomenon, written in larger letters, as the ethical confusion previously described. Weakness or lack of principle creates a general fluidity favourable to novel and even repulsive experiments. All sorts of things traditionally censured as morally, socially, or economically improper and pernicious are shamelessly done. There is simultaneously a tremendous outburst of wild and often stupid theory, seeking to justify novelties already adopted or to recommend innovations even more daring. In no part of the field is there an orthodoxy, a body of principle, strong enough to stand up against this restless questioning and undisciplined speculation, able to distinguish authoritatively true from false, right from wrong. The German version of Fascism, with its explicit advocacy of the Follow my Leader principle, betrays more obviously than the Italian form that it is only a violent cutting of the knot. The mood is that of Wordsworth's lines—'Me this unchartered freedom tires, I feel the weight of chance desires: I long for a repose that ever is the same'. Duty and obedience, blind obedience to the Leader, is the alternative offered and widely approved. Fascism, of course, in Germany claims to have a *Weltanschauung* which will fill the void to which it owed its opportunity, and demands that every German shall be educated in it, but the content of this creed is very slight, and Italian Fascism admits that it is purely opportunist. I cannot see that this violent cutting of the knot can do anything in the long run but aggravate the disease from which it offered release. If the disease was a generally disabling doubt, hysterical assertion without conviction will not cure it. The machinery of representative government which the Fascists have scrapped made evident the fact that no one knew what to do. There was so little clearness as to end and means that none of the committees on which such government rests could evolve any settled policy. In such a situation a committee is an almost insuperable obstacle to action. Fascism pushes these obstacles aside and so formally restores the power of action. But the problem is only transferred to the one who leads, and where shall the leader find his inspiration? He can give the people parade and spectacles and a great show of business, but it soon becomes apparent that after all he knows no better than anyone else what to do. In Germany as in Italy, we are faced by the ultimate prospect of a people (in the pathetic refrain of a song current in 1914), 'all dressed up and no place to go'. The other popular solution of the day, dogmatic Marxism, is also, as it seems to me, a violent cutting of the knot; but it is also certainly much more of a solution, because it is capable of answering every question and it has a constructive long-range scheme of reorganization on which men's hopes may well continue for generations to be fixed. It is therefore capable of lasting as Fascism is not. But apart from the details of the dogma offered, Marxism as we know it is irredeemably dogmatic, and dogma as such is repulsive to any speculative mind. Must we choose, then, we ask with Kant, between scepticism and dogmatism, or is there a third and better way?

II

The only answer to this question, it might seem, which is open to the president of a philosophic society, is an endorsement of the famous thesis which is the centre of Plato's *Republic*.

> Until philosophers are kings, or the kings and princes of this world have the spirit and power of philosophy, and political greatness and wisdom meet in one, and those commoner natures who pursue either to the exclusion of the other are compelled to

stand aside, cities will never have rest from their evils—no, nor
the human race, as I believe—and then only will this our State
have a possibility of life and behold the light of day.

But this is an Aristotelian, not a Platonic Society; and
Aristotle showed reason for thinking that in this as in other
respects Plato seriously overestimated the power of philosophy. I am disposed to agree with Aristotle's criticism; but
in any case before we can profitably consider the possible
contribution of philosophy to the reconstruction of belief, it
is necessary to give some attention to the more general
question, what the power and function of philosophy is.

In a well-known aphorism, F. H. Bradley has said that
'metaphysics is the finding of bad reasons for what we
believe upon instinct'. Bertrand Russell once declared that
'philosophy should show us the hierarchy of our instinctive
beliefs. . . . It should take care to show that, in the form in
which they are finally set forth, our instinctive beliefs do not
clash, but form a harmonious system. There can never be
any reason for rejecting one instinctive belief except that it
clashes with others; thus, if they are found to harmonize,
the whole system becomes worthy of acceptance' (*Prob. of
Phil.*, p. 39). There is no need to examine closely the word
instinct which figures in both statements. I quote these two
very diverse authorities only because they seem to agree on
a point which if true is vital to our present discussion.
Philosophy, they both imply, has its task set to it from
without, by activities quite independent of itself; these
activities are represented as spontaneously generating a set
of beliefs or principles, of which the practitioner need not
apparently even be conscious, which, in any case he is
unable to question, and the principles thus generated are
represented as constituting the philosophic problem. Now
if this, or something like it, is true, it follows that a period
of uncertainty and disorganization in the primary activities
must necessarily be an unproductive period in the second-
ary activity of philosophy. The looms will stand idle for
lack of raw material, or work to little effect because of its
inferior quality. But we have already noticed that at such

times of disorganization in the primary activities the demand for philosophy is exceptionally great. So we get a practical paradox of a familiar type. The demand for philosophy is at a maximum when its possibilities are at a minimum, and vice versa. Just as, on the Stock Exchange, shares are always offered at bargain prices when we have no money to buy them, and when we have the money they are apt to be so dear as to be hardly worth buying.

Let us take once more a fleeting glance at the frontiers of philosophy and natural science. If at any point the enquiries in which the life of science consists break down and come to a stand, I cannot see that the philosopher by means of his philosophy can make any direct contribution to their revival and re-establishment. If it were the case that the sciences rested, even in part, on fundamental premises supplied by philosophy, the situation would be different; but does anyone now believe that this is so? Recent philosophical discussions of physics give no support to any such view. On the contrary, they show the philosopher in this region always as in principle receptive, waiting upon the physicist. It is for the physicist to decide; philosophy can at most criticize. The reason why philosophers intervened was, first, as has already been suggested, because the physicist appeared to be engaged in disavowing what had previously been taken to be their 'instinctive beliefs'—a manoeuvre as suspect to a philosopher as a manipulation of the raw cotton market is to a cotton-spinner; secondly, because physicists in questioning and modifying these fundamentals of theirs were inclined to suggest certain generalizations of the new principle which took them admittedly outside the sphere of physics altogether and were in fact metaphysical theorems. With regard to these excursions into metaphysics, the physicist, of course, was the trespasser, and it was for philosophy to decide, but the decision of the other question rests entirely with the physicist; it is for him to say what principles he needs for the solution of his own problems. The philosopher can only await judgment, and though he may be said to criticize the result, he has no right to impugn the validity of the principles in their own sphere. It should be noted that the restriction of philosophic competence above asserted does not depend upon the acceptance of a Kantian conception of metaphysics. Even if metaphysics in the pre-Kantian sense is possible, it still does not follow that metaphysics can legislate for science. Conceivably the human mind may be able one day to determine what being in general must be; but it is by no means certain that on that basis it would be able to determine what the several spheres of being must be. Aristotle maintained that being was not in that sense a genus, and if that is so, the sciences still retain their autonomy. Anyhow in practice the fact is evident that the scientific world is self governing and will not submit to the dictation of philosophy.

The point I wish to make is merely that a similar restriction of competence debars the philosopher from constructive action in the practical field. The most obvious difference here is that while some philosophers are physicists, all philosophers are to some extent practical men, and as practical men actually take part in establishing and maintaining the standards and principles which as philosophers it is their duty to investigate; but this only makes the confusion of the two sets of questions more likely to occur and more difficult to avoid. And, further, since action is inarticulate, and since the practitioner in any region is only too apt, when he does give an account of his own procedure, to misrepresent himself, there is a kind of gap between conduct and philosophical reflection upon it, which has no parallel in the case of science. There is room here for a variety of descriptive work, recording how the men of a given time and society actually live and act, how their societies are organized, how their political institutions are ordered and administered, and so on. There is room also for all the many kinds of hortatory literature, sermons, tracts, projects of reform, etc., recommending reorganization and revaluation. Both kinds of literature, both the descriptive and the hortatory, are commonly produced by persons who make no claim to be philosophers, and contain in fact a minimum of philosophical reflection. But the philosopher, when his subject is conduct, is seldom careful to remain on his own side of the gap. For one reason or another he commonly prefers to fill it himself. It is even perhaps exceptional to find a work on Ethics or (still more) Politics by a professional philosopher which is to any great extent philosophical in character. Much the greater part of Aristotle's *Ethics*, for instance, is descriptive or analytical of the ethical valuations of contemporary society; a good deal of it is hortatory. Hardly any of it is philosophical. But this is perhaps not a fair instance, since Aristotle did not believe that ethics was a part of philosophy.

My object in the foregoing remarks is not at all to criticize philosophers for their treatment of the problem of conduct; I am charitable enough to suppose that they have good reason for what they do. I only want to show how I understand their performances in this region and to explain something which must, I think, have struck every student of philosophy, viz. the relative impurity of works of practical philosophy. (It is of course precisely this impurity which makes ethics and politics the best gate of entry for the non-philosophical student into the philosophical field.) The point is highly relevant to the present discussion. For by reason of this impurity the moral philosopher does in fact assert ethical values, recommend lines of action, advocate reforms of existing institutions—all things which as a practical man he has a perfect right to do, but none of them in themselves activities pertaining to a philosopher. The philosopher, I should say, in virtue of his philosophy cannot prove anything to be good or bad. If men really think that vice is better than virtue, that justice is a dream or a triviality, that all significant relations between states can be expressed in power equations, philosophy can only register these facts and explore their implications. By cross-examination of those who say these things the philosopher may in fact be able to show that they do not mean what they say. That will no doubt be a useful service, but it is not itself philosophy. It is a preliminary rectification of something offered as a starting-point for philosophical reflection. The refutations of such moral nihilism to be found in philosophical works, as in the *Republic* of Plato, for instance, are largely exercises of this order, i.e. demonstrations that the thesis in question is meaningless. So far as they are not that and really claim to prove, for instance, that virtue is better than vice, they are either question-begging, in the sense that they are substantially only the assertion of a divergent valuation, or what they prove is not what they pretend to prove.

I see no reason at this stage to consider politics separately. I assume that what is said above applies equally in both fields. And I proceed to register the immediate conclusion that if there is scepticism and disorder in the practical field the philosopher is totally unable to remedy it and reconstruct the shattered fabric of belief. If the world asks this of him, it asks something which he cannot give. The very nature of the philosophic task precludes him from any such service. The certainties on which he builds are certainties developed and tested by practical men in the conduct of life. If these are lacking, it is not in his power to create them.

### III

But, as the title of this paper implies, I cannot rest in this negation. I began by pointing to a need and a demand; I went on to explain that in my view the demand is not one that philosophy can meet; what I want to do in conclusion is to show that the philosopher is nevertheless in a position to give some real assistance in the practical field, and to urge therefore on my colleagues the advisability of giving fuller and wider attention to that side of their responsibilities.

In the economy of human thought it seems that philosophy and science (i.e. the complex of the natural sciences) are the natural complements of one another. Being mutually complementary they advance normally, as would be expected, hand in hand. The philosophic synthesis and the scientific analysis are interdependent and inseparable. The sciences make progress by minute subdivision of a field which the philosopher has always to consider as a whole. But this subdivision presupposes a plan of the whole, which the sciences may be said collectively to affirm. Yet this plan, on which they work and which they are said to believe in, is something which they have never had before them at all; it is revealed for the first time by the subsequent efforts of philosophic reflection. It is hardly more than a pattern into which the scientists fall as they go about their business of exploring nature. It comes from no supreme directing brain and is administered by no general staff. It is a pure product of empirical opportunism, and any necessity it may claim is a necessity of fact. Now this pattern or plan is, in fact, constantly being disturbed and developed, but mostly in its minor features only, which represent its adjustment to the more superficial features of nature. The general plan remains over long periods the same, and these minor adjustments leave it unaffected, a reliable foundation for the co-operative labours of the scientific hive. More far-reaching adjustments are at times necessary, and these must of course dislocate research on a more extensive scale, by enforcing revision of its assumptions, and thus endanger to some extent the whole co-operative enterprise. It is at such times that the frontiers between philosophy and science become doubtful, and the philosopher finds himself exceptionally in a position to do some small service to the scientist. Of such crises we may perhaps say that they represent a phase in which, to a greater or lesser extent, a new synthesis has to be made before the work of analysis can profitably continue.

On the practical side, I would suggest, the special responsibilities and opportunities of philosophy depend similarly on the generally recognized fact that social organization means division of labour. Plato, who was one of the first to point this out, immediately demanded and sought to give a rational justification for such division, and his scheme for a rational division of labour became a scheme for a complete social revolution. But neither philosophy nor science is in a position to say authoritatively how social functions ought to be allotted, though each may offer facts and theories which are easily turned into criticism of the actual allotment. Here too we have, in fact, cooperative work on a large scale based on a plan for which no one is responsible—a pattern into which human life has somehow fallen. And it sometimes seems that society can only keep running smoothly and happily so long as everyone takes the plan so much for granted that no one even asks what it is. As soon as attention is directed to it, a justification is of course demanded, and little discussion is needed before every citizen and every group of citizens is profoundly convinced that the plan gives him (or it) a position in society wholly incommensurate with his (or their) deserts. Yet more and more in the modern world social self-consciousness increases; more and more eagerly men search for some principle on which social functions shall be justly distributed, some principle of higher authority than economic necessity or historical accident. In our own day, the consciously planned society is often said to exist or to be coming into existence. But it is probable that no individual and no society can plan more than a very small fraction of its life, however important that small fraction may be.

From the social point of view each one of us is a highly specialized worker, tied to his own little niche in the general scheme. In that respect we are products of an analysis for which as individuals we are not responsible and over which we have no control. But decisions have to be taken for society as a whole, with due regard to all the varied interests which it comprises, and this synthetic activity is of course the subject-matter of politics. In the name of the democratic principle an attempt is made to induce every adult citizen to take a part in this work of synthesis, and so far as this is successful he gets some understanding of the whole and of his place in it. This is clearly a valuable corrective of the inevitable specialization of function, and that is one good argument for democratic institutions. But there is another reason for aiming at a democracy which perhaps goes deeper. Democracy may be regarded as essentially the product of political and social empiricism. If it were the case that the human mind could formulate completely and indisputably all the principles and possibilities of human nature, the argument would be impossible to resist that one wise man, or a group of such, ought to be put in charge of each society; but this is not so, and the imposture of collective wisdom, of which anti-democrats talk, is less of a swindle than the imposture of individual inspiration, which is their alternative, when it is not anarchy. The empiricist is modest in his claims for reason, and it is not collective wisdom that he means to assert when he supports democracy. He is looking for an arrangement by which the natural growth of a society will be as little obstructed as possible, by which at the same time all constructive ideas can find easy expression, considering that the human intellect at its highest is mainly exercised in guiding and correcting movements which it did not originate.

These remarks lead me a little aside from my main point, but they are not irrelevant, since they should explain briefly how I understand the work of political synthesis on which the health of societies so largely and increasingly depends. The work itself must be left mainly, even in a democratic state, to professional politicians. The question is whether in this extremely difficult and critical work they might not be given more effective help than they now receive, and whether in particular the philosopher might not help them.

It is not a question of expert advice. The politician is himself an expert in the political machine and its possibilities, and experts in any desired field are easily found or made. These and the specialist social sciences, like economics, belong to the analytic distribution of social effort and represent material which politics exists to synthesize. It is a question of assistance in the work of synthesis itself. The question is, where is this to be found? It seems to me that there are only two established disciplines from which the required assistance could possibly be expected. These are history and philosophy; and of the two philosophy appears to have much the greater possibilities. Both have it in their power to restore to due proportion a perspective distorted, as that of the practical man must always tend to be, by the pressure of present emergency. Both can contribute effectively to the achievement of that distance and detachment, which is so necessary a condition of genuine statesmanship. Some men, no doubt, of high ability, have a constitutional aversion to philosophy, and for them history will be the only resource. But where this aversion does not exist, and both roads lie open, the superiority lies surely with philosophy. For the benefits derived from history are mostly indirect; its only essential service is in the close neighbourhood of the problems at issue, and generally in bringing home that continuity of present, past and future which makes Society, in Burke's words, a partnership 'between those who are living, those who are dead, and those who are to be born'. Otherwise the reader has to make his connexions mostly for himself, and in so doing he is apt to fall into questionable and even dangerous analogies. But in a philosophical analysis of society the subject-matter is the more permanent aspects of those very problems which the politician is himself employed in handling, and the mode of argumentation used is largely of the same order as that which he himself in facing these problems is forced to use. Philosophy, I mean, by its refusal to abstract and its insistence on taking everything into account, is forced to put aside all idea of exact calculation and mathematical demonstration in respect of its central assertions, and the practical man or statesman, however much he may employ these in the preliminaries, has in the end to do the same.

If I am right in the view of philosophy which I have outlined above, if its primary task is to exhibit the constitutive principles of theoretical and other human activities, which came into existence without its help and are in no sense subject to its rulings, it follows no doubt that these activities will continue to go their own way, and there can be no guarantee that their progress will always be perfectly orderly and consistent, or wholly satisfactory to the philosophic critic. But it does not follow that philosophic criticism is of no assistance to their progress: on the contrary it may still be at times almost indispensable. For philosophy on this showing has the task of expounding to them on the evidence of their activities what their fundamental beliefs are, and that task, which may seem almost otiose when all is going well, becomes important as soon as things begin to go badly. When the foundations are shaking, it is as well to know what they are. These considerations apply in my view over the whole field of philosophy, but they apply, for reasons already given, with especial force on the practical side. If philosophers were to cease, *per impossibile*, to take any interest in the progress of the natural sciences, no very serious harm would result. The scientific world would respond by evolving, as to a large extent it already does, its own critical apparatus. But in the practical field proverbially the sign of strength is silence, and a call to reflective criticism is resented as an interference with the practical programme and a solvent of effort. The man of action has little leisure or inclination to discuss the principles on which he acts. Therefore his critical thinking has to be done largely for him. And my case is that a social philosophy is needed for this purpose—a philosophical synthesis specializing in the social field as philosophers also specialize in science or the field of art. This post-war generation is, I think, in urgent need of such a synthesis. Our young men and women are attracted in large and probably increasing numbers to the Marxist creed, not so much because it is adequate and theoretically unanswerable, as because it is the only coherent body of doctrine that they can find. Many, probably most of them, are not philosophers, and possibly they are rather repelled than attracted by the philosophic side of the creed. But that side of it is very important and its adequate discussion is a real need. What is wanted is a philosophic discipline, encouraging and promoting the careful exposition and discussion of the presuppositions of social organization on every side. No such discipline exists in this country at present. If it existed it might of course tend to the endorsement of the Marxist case; but if so it would be a more intelligent Marxism than we commonly meet today. But those who believe, as I do, that the Marxist position contains fundamental falsehood, will be confident that it would be able to show those who are drawn towards it a better way—not by preaching an alternative ideal, or by inventing a rival Utopia, but by showing them on the evidence of the actual achievements of humanity what man's fundamental beliefs really are, and by showing further how little of all this is honoured in the Marxist solution, and how much is excluded. I take Marxism only as a highly topical example. My point is that our generation is not being given in these matters the tools necessary for coming to a sound critical judgment, and that philosophy alone has the power to give them these tools. When men do not know the faith by which they live, they will be apt inadvertently to betray it.

# 7

## Can Philosophy Determine What is Ethically or Socially Valuable?

The problem raised by this question is to my mind fundamentally the problem how far and in what sense the philosopher is in a position to give assistance to the practical man in his action; in particular, whether he is rightly expected to prescribe the end or goal or principle of action for men as moral individuals, or for societies as responsible for organizing and directing the lives of their members. I answer the question with a qualified negative, i.e. I think that the philosopher can be of assistance to the practical man, but not in the way suggested. Perhaps a further personal explanation may be in order, since it will show how the question in fact arose and why I am asked to open the discussion though my answer is to this extent negative.

At the beginning of this session I wrote a paper for the Aristotelian Society under the title 'The Need for a Social Philosophy', concerned largely with this very point. In the course of that paper I called attention to the fact that large portions of the books written by philosophers on ethics and politics are not strictly philosophical in character: to a large extent they are descriptive, occupied in recording relevant experiences, and in much of the rest they are apt to be hortatory, occupied in recommending this or that reform or line of action. From a strictly philosophical point of view there is a high degree of impurity in such works, which may be generally desirable and justifiable and certainly makes them more attractive to the non-philosophic reader, but is apt to cause confusion in the reader's mind as to the task of philosophy and the contribution to be expected from it. I went on as follows:

> by reason of this impurity the moral philosopher does in fact assert ethical values, recommend lines of action, advocate reforms of existing institutions—all things which as a practical man he has a perfect right to do, but none of them in themselves activities pertaining to a philosopher. The philosopher, I should say, in virtue of his philosophy cannot prove anything to be good or bad. If men really think that vice is better than virtue, that justice is a dream or a triviality, that all significant relations between states can be expressed in power equations, philosophy can only register these facts and explore their implications. By cross-examination of those who say these things the philosopher may in fact be able to show that they do not mean what they say. That will no doubt be a useful service, but it is not itself philosophy. It is a preliminary rectification of something offered as a starting-point for philosophical reflection. The refutations of such moral nihilism to be found in philosophical works, as in the *Republic* of Plato, for instance, are largely exercises of this order, i.e., demonstrations that the thesis in question is meaningless. So far as they are not that and really claim to prove, for instance, that virtue is better than vice, they are either question-begging, in the sense that they are substantially only the assertion of a divergent valuation, or what they prove is not what they pretend to prove (pp. 11–12).

My task in opening this discussion is to re-state and explain these contentions, and explanation is clearly desirable on two main points—(1) as to the conception of philosophy presupposed, (2) as to the relation of philosophical reflection to the grounds of practical judgment and decision.

I. *Philosophy and its task.* I agree substantially with the conception of the philosopher's task, which Bertrand Russell adopted some twenty-five years ago when he wrote his *Problems of Philosophy*.

> Philosophy (he said) should show us the hierarchy of our

instinctive beliefs . . . It should take care to show that, in the form in which they are finally set forth, our instinctive beliefs do not clash, but form a harmonious system. There can never be any reason for rejecting one instinctive belief except that it clashes with others; thus, if they are found to harmonize, the whole system becomes worthy of acceptance.

Russell had in mind chiefly, when he wrote those words, fundamental common-sense assumptions, such as that material bodies exist. Whether he would have attached any special value to the word 'instinctive', which I do not much like, I do not know; nor do I know what else, if anything, he would have asked the philosopher to do besides exploring and exhibiting the system of these beliefs. When he says that no such belief can legitimately be rejected except on the ground of its inconsistency with others, he seems to imply that the philosopher's constructive task is exhausted in this. However that may be, I see no reason why the conception should not be generalized so as to include not merely the practical presuppositions of common sense, to which the word 'instinct' is not inappropriate, but also, e.g., the principles of induction, which he goes on later in the same book to investigate, and the complex assumptions which underlie the scientific interpretation of nature, in regard to which the word 'instinct' seems to be rather out of place. And with that extension, if it is an extension, and with a request for a better word than 'instinctive', I am prepared to accept the description as fitting the philosophic task.

Philosophy, as I understand it, is essentially a reflective activity of thought, in contact with reality, so far as reality is other than mind, not directly but through primary and pre-existing mental reactions to it. These primary activities are of various kinds, but all alike come into existence without the philosopher's assistance and go their way independently of him. He has no power or title to regulate or control them. Each of them has its own actuating principles and its own fundamental constitutive beliefs. These last are not a set of clearly formulated principles, which can be set out once for all, like the axioms of Euclid, before the activity begins, but rather principles and beliefs developed experimentally as the activity develops, and justified for the experimenter by the success of the experiments in which they are operative. The task of the philosopher is (1) to determine the precise character of the principles, (2) to pursue their implications, (3) to consider all questions arising from the inter-relation of the pre-suppositions of human thought, theoretical and practical, in its different fields of exercise. The first of these three tasks calls for special familiarity with a particular field, and thus accounts for a certain degree of specialization on the part of philosophers. The specialization may be lasting or it may be, so to speak, periodical. One philosopher is specially at home in the field of science (or the philosopher at one period devotes himself to this side of thought); another philosopher (or the philosopher at another time) concentrates on art or religion or history or on the problems of the practical life in ethics and politics; and in this way are produced philosophical treatments of these departments. But, if the treatment is to be philosophical, the specialization cannot be absolute. In executing the first of his three tasks the philosopher must have in mind the second and the third; for it is his business, as a philosopher, not merely to understand the procedure of the artist or the scientist, but to procure an insight into the nature of reality in its universality. This differentiates his work from that of the specialist proper. An artist will sometimes discuss the principles of his art, an experienced politician will attempt to expound the lessons of his experience and the principles which have guided him in his work: either of them may in fact have something of the philosopher in his composition, and if so that will complicate the formula; but primarily, and so far as they are true to their own specialities, each will have in mind his own successes and what made them possible: each will be making a contribution to his own speciality with a view to improving its practice. The philosopher is facing in the opposite direction. What interests him is not the consequences of these principles in operation, but their presuppositions: his question is, What must the world be to make this possible? To say this is, of course, only to generalize the theorem concerning the opposite movements of philosophic and scientific thought which Plato formulated in his *Republic*. In terms of the triple task formulated above it means that while both the specialist proper in his reflective moments and the philosopher will appear to face the second of the questions enumerated, viz., that of the implications of the principles, they will be concerned, so far as each is true to his nature, with a different set of implications. The considerations which specially concern the philosopher may be called the metaphysical implications, and these do not concern the practitioner as such.

I would only add, with no emphasis, because it is not very relevant here, that it seems to me to be clear that the main philosophical controversies are incidental to the third of the tasks set out above. The successes of science, for example, are represented as requiring or implying a materialistic interpretation of nature; action, on the other hand, and the principles of moral judgment upon it, are represented as demanding a conception of the material as malleable by a will which is not material. Thus there is a conflict, real or apparent, between the implications of two different kinds of human experience, out of which prolonged disputes connected with terms like materialism, the freedom of the will, etc., are born. To accept such a conflict as inevitable and irreconcilable would be to surrender the faith on which knowledge depends, and therefore in attempting to reinterpret the rival theses so as to remove their apparent conflict the philosopher is undertaking a necessary task, which has to be performed if the several activities which are in apparent conflict are not to be paralysed by fundamental doubts.

II. *The practical field.* If the foregoing definition of the philosophic task is correct, it follows at once that the first duty of the philosopher in any field which he may enter, and therefore specifically in the practical field which is here in question, is to determine a question of fact. If a normative science is one that sets out to formulate ideals which are in no determinable relation to current practice, his is not a normative science. With ideals and principles of action he is certainly concerned, and equally certainly these ideals and principles of action are not always and everywhere effective in action, but if they are nowhere effective it is difficult to see what right they have to their name. His first task is to determine by the appropriate evidence what the operative principles of conduct actually are and what are the limits of their operation. It is his business to find out what is thought obligatory, not what ought to be thought obligatory; what is considered good, not what it is good to consider good. It is no more his business to put himself in the place of the agent or politician, and think out his problem for him afresh, than it is his place to go into the scientific laboratory and attempt a new solution of the scientist's problem. He is concerned only with the reflective interpretation of a given activity, and such interpretation must start, like any interpretation, from determination of fact. It merely happens that in this case the relevant facts are essentially valuations; and this creates a confusion in some people's minds, who cannot conceive a valuation as a fact requiring accurate definition and analysis.

Another source of confusion here arises from a tendency, which seems to be natural to the unsophisticated human mind, to a utilitarian interpretation of conduct. If all differences of practical valuation are reducible in the last resort to differences in acceptability between the probable results of action, then the obvious conception of ethical and political theory is the conception of it as directed to determining the general considerations on which such acceptability depends or should depend. Men will thus go to ethics and politics (to borrow Aristotle's metaphor) like archers in search of a mark. Nearer objectives they have no doubt in plenty, based on blind instinct, example, tribal custom, and other questionable foundations; but to bring order into their lives and achieve the full freedom of a planned life they want an ultimate objective in reference to which these others may be systematized and regulated. On this view the philosophical theorist is conceived as thinking on precisely the same lines as the man of action, but as carrying the thought further and deeper than the man of action is willing or able to carry it. He will be telling the practical man, who has no leisure to complete the answer to his own perpetual question, what in the long run is really worth having. But even if the utilitarian view is correct, this conception of ethics and politics does not necessarily follow. It may still be the case that the philosopher has no authority from his philosophy for pronouncing that this is better than that, and that when he propounds a definition of the human good, the evidence for the truth and adequacy of this conception is to be found in the more limited judgments of the man of action, of which it is the continuation and justification. In this case the philosopher will after all be occupied in substance in deciding a question of fact: he will be telling the practical man what he really is aiming at all the time. Aristotle's own final conclusion was really that this is what the ethical and political philosopher actually does.

But, it will be said, even if the first step is the determination of fact, which may well be true, the philosopher cannot surely stop at that. Surely it is his obvious duty to criticize these judgments of value, to correct errors and misapprehensions, to recommend the right principles of action and so contribute to the making of a better and happier world.

This is the type of objection which in one form or another is always brought against anyone who puts forward such a conception of practical philosophy as I am now advancing. I have come to the conclusion that its real root is the failure to realize what a difficult task in the practical field this initial task (as I have called it) of determining the facts is, and how little therefore relatively remains to be done when it is satisfactorily accomplished. The idea that the commands and principles of morality are as plain as a pikestaff may be a convenience to rulers and teachers and other lovers of docility, but it is a long way from the truth and a serious obstacle to anyone who wishes to establish a sound practical philosophy. The material which must form the empirical basis of any theory is rich and various. It consists of acts and judgments—acts of our own and of other persons, judgments upon acts and projects of action of our own and of other persons. Each of these acts and judgments is essentially atomic and isolated, as the judgments of aesthetic appreciation are also atomic and isolated. Each has reference to a particular performance and situation, and no other. Consequently there may be any degree of inconsequence and inconsistency between them. How many people judge themselves and other persons by the same measures, or hold consistently to one standard of judgment over a period? Further, the specifically moral factor in action and in judgment is so inextricably mixed up with other factors that its separate operation is not in fact conceivable and its theoretical isolation is a matter of extreme difficulty. The moral diagnosis of any act involves necessarily the ascription of motives to the agent, and how can we, who find by experience that we cannot pronounce confidently as to our own motives, identify with any confidence the motives of someone else? There is obviously an enormous gap between this chaotic material and the tidy ethical systems which philosophers offer us as the result of their reflection upon it. The philosopher does not trouble much to show the steps by which from that starting-point he arrived at this result. It often seems as though he had been content to generalize from his own limited practical experience, assuming that it was typical or authoritative. But whether the field from which the material is drawn is wide or narrow, it seems clear that the determination of the facts, which is the first step, is no simple straightforward matter, but a difficult and complicated undertaking.

My first answer then is that the question of fact, the question what are the ideals and principles actually operative in the field of practice, is by itself a question of sufficient magnitude to occupy justifiably the main part of an investigator's attention. My second answer is that such correction and criticism of current practice and belief as is logically justifiable will be given implicitly in the attempt at a systematic exposition of the facts. Everything turns here on the question how the valuations on which the decisions of the agent or statesman depend are established or confirmed. If they are capable of systematic *a priori* exposition and proof, then I suppose the philosopher might undertake this and so formulate a body of doctrine, like Locke's Law of Nature, which would be 'an eternal rule to all men, legislators as well as others'. By it as standard he could judge the actual practice of legislators and others, and show wherein it fell short. But I see no reason to suppose that any such body of *a priori* law is attainable. A more laborious empirical method has therefore to be devised. This means that the would-be theorist of conduct has to face the mass of material above described and attempt to reduce it to some degree of order. He has to show that this multiplicity is at bottom a unity, that this unorganized sequence of decisions and judgments has none the less its own inner organization and can be plausibly regarded as the expression of a single principle or of a few fundamental ideas which are in intelligible relation to one another. Now the fundamental principle of any empirical method, as John Stuart Mill rightly pointed out, is this: 'we have no ulterior test to which we subject experience in general; but we make experience its own test'. Mill was thinking of the scientific exploration of nature. The principle is no doubt sound there, but it is far more directly and obviously applicable when the object to be tested or judged is an expression of human effort and reason. Every such manifestation of mind must necessarily be an attempt to achieve something which is not in fact fully achieved. To state its aim and motive is to state a fact: this is what the agent, the painter, the poet, was actually aiming at. To describe the achievement is also to state a fact: this is what he actually achieved. The perceived interval between the first and the second of these two parts is a main ground of favourable and unfavourable judgment upon actions and upon the products of art.

The only way we have of *persuading* other people (as

distinct from inducing them by threats, bribery, bullying, etc.) to desist from some course of action is to show them that its continuation will obstruct certain things which they also desire, or that it implies the acceptance of principles and beliefs irreconcilable with those implied by other actions to which they are also committed. The practical man generally, and the politician in particular, is very sensitive to charges of inconsistency, and will resort to the most transparent devices to prove the straightness of a most obviously tortuous course of action. If it were not for this 'instinctive belief' in practical consistency, if practical decisions were really as independent of one another as they often seem to be, the reflective analysis of the philosopher, however interesting and necessary as theory, would be of no importance for practice. But given this demand and belief, his possible influence is very great, and arises directly from the exposition of fact in the sense already explained. Let me illustrate this by an example from political theory. Locke in his *Civil Government* says that 'the great and chief end of men uniting into commonwealths' is the preservation of their property, i.e. 'life, liberty, and estate'. With this principle in his hand he proceeds to condemn this constitutional or other provision and approve that. He thinks that his starting point is in human reason, i.e., in that which is evident *a priori*, and would probably demur to the suggestion that it is taken from the facts themselves. Yet surely in truth what he did was to reflect on the principles and practice of government in England—and no doubt in other countries—as known to him, and in the course of that reflection convinced himself that the more permanent and constructive features of that government implied fundamentally the observance of some such principle, while disorder, disaster, and weakness entered in so often as public action was taken which implied its suspension or rejection. And having thus obtained his principle from the facts he uses it to judge the facts. What is accepted is accepted as necessary and helpful, what is rejected is rejected as harmful and obstructive to this 'great and chief end'. For a long time after it was written, Locke's work was very influential in the political field. The extent of Locke's influence was due, not to theoretical conceptions, already half obsolete, like the law of nature and the social contract, but to the superb judgment with which he discerned and expounded for his contemporaries the central currents in the turbulent stream of events through which he lived. It was this that gave him his hold on future practice, and enabled his teaching to work for its strengthening and purification.

*Conclusion.* The practical values, in my view, are created, sustained, and developed by practitioners who are in direct contact with the external world at the requisite point. Theirs is the only authoritative and responsible judgment as to what is valuable, and all generalization upon the nature of value and the valuable has to recognize its dependence upon them. New and unforeseen developments at these points of direct contact are always possible, and in such cases it will always be difficult to tell wilful caprice from fruitful innovation. Rules of a kind may be formulated to govern practice, but they have no theoretical foundation: they are essentially generalizations from practice, without power to bind future practice, and without value except for beginners. Reflective analysis by the practitioner of his own practice is no doubt in some degree a persistent element in the practice and contributes to its efficiency, especially by increasing its coherence and consistency. More elaborate attempts at such analysis are undertaken occasionally by the practitioners themselves and persistently by philosophers in treatises devoted to the subject. In their nature these efforts are identical with those of the self-conscious practitioner, and their possible service to practice is of the same order as that of his reflections. But when they are philosophical they have a further aim. They are not directed essentially to the improvement of practice, but to the definition of the principles of practice with a view to clearing up the nature of the world and man's place in it. In any case these re-flective efforts are not directly creative: they do not open up new spheres of value: that function is reserved for the practitioner. They are not legislative, producing principles binding on the practitioner: the practice is autonomous. The only sense in which philosophy can be said to determine what is ethically or politically valuable is this, that in its critical examination of the practice and in its exposition of its principles it is attempting to make explicit and evident assumptions as to the nature of good which are for the practitioner largely concealed within the concrete detail of his judgments and decisions. It is only so far as the man of action is reflective that the philosophical analysis links up directly with his thought: towards the answer to his primary question, What shall I do?, philosophy contributes directly nothing.

# *Index*

ACTION, agent and spectator judgements, 54 f.
  and agent, 54
  and expression, 56
  and a general conception of the will as the basis of moral judgements and values, 66–7
  and intentions, 54
  and rationality, 56
  its results and character, 54–6, 58–9
AFFECTION, 9
  and aesthetic appreciation, 46–7
  its concentration on the particular and the individual, 41–3
  contrasted with desire, 40 f.
  its involvement with desire (love and lust, property and wealth, loyalty and jingoism), 43–4
  and knowledge of persons, 45–9
  and morality, 47
  and thought, 40 f.
ANSCOMBE, G. E. M., 5 n.
ARISTOTLE, 6, 10, 15, 19, 73, 75, 77, 84–8, 91–7, 106, 108–9, 122–3
  *Ethics*, 94, 109
  *Metaphysics*, 93
  *Politics*, 94
AURELIUS, MARCUS, 7, 68

BENEVOLENCE, 68
BOSWELL'S *LIFE OF JOHNSON*, 46, 99
BRADLEY, F. H., 4–5, 75–6, 106
BROWNING, ROBERT, 77, 82

BURKE, EDMUND, 22
BUTLER, BISHOP, 59, 71

CATEGORICAL IMPERATIVE, 95
CHARACTER, in action, 3, 54–6, 59
CONSCIENCE, 53
CONSEQUENCES, 10, 81
CONSISTENCY, regard for, 126–7

DARWIN, CHARLES, 90
DEMOCRACY, 112–13
DESIRE, 8
  contrasted with affection, 40 f.
  and the desirable, 36–7
  its inadequacy as an account of human action, 39–40
  its involvement with affection, 42–4
  and rationality, 38
  its relation to thought, 34 f.
  its relative character and generality, 9, 38
DODINGTON, GEORGE BUBB, 82–3, 98

ENDS, See 'Means and Ends'
EUCLID, 119

FACT AND VALUE, 6
FALSIFICATION OF FACTS, 11–13
FASCISM, 104–5
FOOT, PHILIPPA, 5 n.
FRENCH REVOLUTION, 22, 41

129

GODWIN, WILLIAM, 94
GOLDEN MEAN, the, 6–7, 82 f.
 its minor significance for ethics, 98
 its relation to Aristotle's analysis of
  sensation, 86
 its relation to art, 85, 88–9
 its relation to Greek teleology, 94 f.
 its relation to health, 85–6
 its relation to morality, 87–90
 its relation to self-sacrifice and self-
  denial, 95 f.
 its relation to theories of evolution,
  90–1
GREEN, T. H., 4–5, 17 n., 18–19, 75

HARE, R. M., 7 n.
HALIFAX'S *The Character of a
 Trimmer*, 83, 98
HAZLITT, WILLIAM, 100
HEDONISTS, 52
HERACLEITUS, 86
HISTORY AND PHILOSOPHY,
 113–14
HOBBES, THOMAS, 44
HOBHOUSE, LEONARD, 101
HUMAN BEHAVIOUR, desire,
 thought, affection, 49–50

INTENTIONS, 54, 81
INTUITION, 10, 81

JOHNSON'S *PRAYERS AND MEDI-
 TATIONS*, 99
JOYCE, JAMES, 13

KANT, IMMANUEL, 19, 47, 64,
 103, 105
KHAN, GENGHIS, 13

LOCKE, JOHN, 38
 *CIVIL GOVERNMENT*, 126

MACAULAY, THOMAS
 BABINGTON, LORD, 100
MARXISM, 13, 105, 115–16
MATERIALISM, 91
MEANS AND ENDS, 15
 and artistic activity, 12–14, 60–1
 the end justifies the means, 58
 the inadequacy of the distinction for

 ethics, 2 f., 19 f., 27–8, 57 f.,
  60–1, 70 f., 77–8
 no ultimate ends, 57–8
MILL, JAMES, 103
MILL, JOHN STUART, 74, 103,
 125
MILTON, JOHN, 84
MORAL DILEMMAS, 9–10
MORALITY, as an additional prin-
 ciple of discrimination, 27–8
MORALITY AND ART, 29–31
MORAL NIHILISM, 110
MORAL VALUES, 10
MORGAN, LLOYD, 90

NEEDS, 5–6, 10
NIETZSCHE, 13

PAUL, ST., 13
PHILLIPS, D. Z., 7 n.
PHILOSOPHY AND ITS RELA-
 TION TO CONDUCT, 11 f.,
 55; 99 f., 106 f.
 the hierarchy of instinctive beliefs,
  118–19
 its impurities, 109 f., 117–18
 its metaphysical concern, 120–1
 its positive task, 110 f.
 the principles underlying human
  action, 12 f., 114 f., 122–3, 124 f.,
  127
 the tendency to generalise, 123–4
PHILOSOPHY AND SCIENCE, 11,
 101–2, 107–8
PLATO, 43, 59, 84–5, 89, 91, 105,
 110–11, 121
 *Phaedo*, 91
 *Republic*, 105, 110, 121
 *Timaeus*, 89
POSITIVE THEORY OF HUMAN
 NATURE, 5
PURPOSE, and art, 21–6
 definition of, 17–18
 will not yield 'good' and 'bad', 73–4
 limitations of as an account of
  human action, 20 f., 72
 and morality, 26 f., 79–81
 excludes motive from moral judgement, 74–5

# Index

PURPOSE—*continued*
  will not yield 'right' and 'wrong', 73
  its relevance for moral action, 78–9
  ultimate, 16–17
PURPOSE AND RATIONALITY, 15 f.
  the levels above them (art, morality, religion), 17
  the levels below them (instinct, appetite, etc.), 16 f., 70–1

RATIONALITY, See 'Action' and 'Purpose and Rationality'
RHEES, RUSH, 9 n.
RUSSELL, BERTRAND, 106, 118–19

SCEPTICISM (in the mid-thirties of this century), 101–5
  in conduct, 102–3
  in politics and sociology, 103–5

in science and metaphysics, 102–3
SELF IN MORAL CONSIDERATIONS, 7–8, 68–9
SELF-CONDEMNATION, 53
SELF-JUDGEMENT AND IMAGINATION, 51–2
SELF-LOVE, 71
SELF-REALISATION, 4, 18, 28–9, 60–5, 75–8
SMUTS, GENERAL, 90–2
  *Holism and Evolution*, 90–3
SOCRATES, 91
SPINOZA, 69, 75

TAYLOR, A. E., 16 n.

UTILITARIANISM, 5, 10, 52, 54, 95, 102

WARD, JAMES, 101
WATSON, W., 31 n.
WITTGENSTEIN, LUDWIG, 9, 9 n.